# George Eliot in Love

ALSO BY BRENDA MADDOX

*Beyond Babel: New Directions in Communications*
*The Half-Parent: Living with Other People's Children*
*Who's Afraid of Elizabeth Taylor? A Myth of Our Time*
*The Marrying Kind: Homosexuality and Marriage*
*Nora: The Life of Nora Joyce*
*D. H. Lawrence: The Story of a Marriage*
*Yeats's Ghosts: The Secret Life of W. B. Yeats*
*Rosalind Franklin: The Dark Lady of DNA*
*Maggie: The First Lady*
*Freud's Wizard: The Enigma of Ernest Jones*

# GEORGE ELIOT IN LOVE

*Brenda Maddox*

palgrave
macmillan

GEORGE ELIOT IN LOVE
Copyright © Brenda Maddox, 2009, 2010.
All rights reserved.

First published in London as *George Eliot: Novelist, Lover, Wife* in 2009 by HarperPress.

First Published in the United States in 2010 by PALGRAVE MACMILLAN®—a division of St. Martin's Press LLC, 175 Fifth Avenue, New York, NY 10010.

Palgrave Macmillan is the global academic imprint of the above companies and has companies and representatives throughout the world.

Palgrave® and Macmillan® are registered trademarks in the United States, the United Kingdom, Europe and other countries.

ISBN 978–0–230–10518–8

Library of Congress Cataloging-in-Publication Data is available from the Library of Congress.

A catalogue record of the book is available from the British Library.

Design by Newgen Imaging Systems, Ltd., Chennai, India

First Palgrave Macmillan edition: October 2010

10 9 8 7 6 5 4 3 2 1

Printed in the United States of America.

*For John, as always*

# CONTENTS

# INTRODUCTION

"Did she have a very unhappy life?" someone asked me.

No.

What follows is a love story. George Eliot, born Mary Anne Evans, was a plain woman and able journalist who never expected happiness. Yet she found great and lasting love with one of the cleverest Englishmen of his day, George Henry Lewes. It was he who persuaded her to try writing fiction. She had never written a novel before she went to live with Lewes in 1854; after his death in 1878 she never wrote another.

Hers is also a success story. As George Eliot, she became such a best-selling author that the rise to riches is part of her triumph, and Lewes's. To give readers some idea of the value of their earnings, I have included in a few places the rough equivalent in twenty-first-century dollars—keeping in mind that currency values are hard to apply to a society so long ago.

Her life was one of continual changes of name. In my text, I refer to her by the name and spelling she was using at each stage of her life. When they were too many and varied, I use "Marian." I also follow, with a few exceptions, her custom of referring to women friends by their first name and men friends by their last.

The past is another country, impossible to approach without the condescension of hindsight. With divorce, cohabitation, and illegitimacy now commonplace, imaginative effort is needed to appreciate the suffering caused to Marian Evans by the impossibility of marrying the man with whom she shared her life. Lewes, by allowing his legal wife's illegitimate children to be registered under his name, had effectively "condoned" her adultery and therefore could never divorce.

Nothing is harder to understand today than the succession of illnesses from which the Leweses (as the couple called themselves) suffered. Most of the "cures" they tried are now risible. One thing is certain; the author believed what she wrote in her journal in March 1866: "We have so much happiness in our love and uninterrupted companionship that we must accept our miserable bodies as our share of mortal ill."

Hers was a noble and moving life. Her happiness was real and her achievement great and enduring.

*Brenda Maddox*
*London 2009*

*Chapter One*

# FATHER'S LITTLE WENCH (1819–1832)

"But were another childhood-world my share, I would be born a little sister there."
—George Eliot, "Brother and Sister" sonnets, 1874

HER FACE WAS her fortune. When their second daughter was born on November 22, 1819, Robert and Christiana Evans could see at a glance that she would find it hard to fulfill a girl's primary task: to find a husband; she would have to make her own way in life. The heavy, irregular features resembling her father's were there from the start: large, drooping nose, long chin, prominent jaw. Decades later, when she had become a famous novelist, many would attempt to describe her odd appearance. George Eliot, the young Henry James wrote to his father in 1870, was "magnificently ugly, deliciously hideous." But James quickly noticed (as her parents seem not to have done) that "in this vast ugliness resides a most powerful beauty which, in a very few minutes steals forth and charms the mind."

Mary Anne Evans was born into the middle class of Middle England, in Warwickshire, at South Farm, outside the town of Nuneaton. She was third of the five children of Robert and Christiana, his second wife. The twin sons who arrived fourteen months later died shortly after birth. Mary Anne's mother never recovered. She was chronically ill and depressed, and being left with the unattractive little girl as her last child only made matters worse. Mary Anne unfortunately inherited both her mother's poor health and low spirits.

Robert Evans was land agent for the Arbury estate, which stood on the wooded fringes of Nuneaton. Situated over Warwickshire's richest coalfield, Nuneaton was four miles from Coventry, an industrial, once-medieval city southeast of larger and newer Birmingham. The railway would not reach Coventry or Birmingham until 1836.

When Mary Anne was only a few months old, the family moved to Griff House, on the edge of the Arbury estate. Griff was a spacious, eight-bedroom redbrick house with a cobbled courtyard, ivy-covered walls, and large chimney pots. Its grounds held numerous barns, stables, dairy sheds, and what was called "the Round Pond."

A reminder that there was a larger world came twice a day, at ten in the morning and three in the afternoon, when the stage coach rumbled along the Coventry Road, past the Griff gates on one side and a quarry on the other.

The rest of the time, the residents of the Arbury estate lived within its seven-thousand-acre universe of farms, forests, and mines. Running through the property was the canal that carried coal from the mines into Coventry. Mary Anne's strong feelings about the dangers of water so vividly expressed in *The Mill on the Floss* perhaps originated here, with the pond and the canal so nearby.

Before the Reform Act of 1832, England was governed by its landowning class. Five percent of the population owned seventy-nine percent of the land. This landed gentry also held most of the votes in the House of Commons. Many places of rapid growth, like Birmingham, had no representation at all, while virtually unpopulated electoral districts sent a Member to Parliament. Seats in these "rotten" boroughs (those of fewer than two thousand people) and "pocket" boroughs (where patrons chose the Members) were controlled by the local landowners, who sold or gave them out at their whim.

As a young man, Robert Evans had been an artisan, good with his hands, especially at carpentry. His skills soon secured him a place in this fixed hierarchy, although he was very conscious that his wife's social status was slightly higher than his because her father owned a small property. Even so, as a manager, Evans stood well above a simple farmer or weaver. Land agency, or estate management, was a decidedly middle-class occupation. The job demanded skill and knowledge, and Evans was one of the best. Mary Anne later claimed that he was "unique amongst land agents for his manifold knowledge and experience," which saved his employers the cost of hiring experts for surveying, excavating, bookkeeping, and making various decisions about property ownership. Evans, physically strong and commercially shrewd, was indispensable to the Newdigate family, who employed him.

Evans's loyalty to the Newdigates was unshakable. He followed his master in always voting Conservative, and his first wife, Harriet Poynton, had been a lady's maid on the Newdigate staff. The couple had two children, Robert and Frances (or Fanny), but Harriet died giving birth to their third child (who also died) in 1809.

Arbury Hall, the center of Evans's world, was the seat of Francis Parker Newdigate. As plain Francis Parker, he had inherited the estate in 1806 from a baronet cousin, Sir Roger Newdigate. Taking Newdigate as his own name, he moved south to Nuneaton from his estate at Kirk Hallam in Derbyshire and brought Robert Evans with him. The Evans family, originally from Wales, had lived in Derbyshire for many generations before this, and a brother remained in Kirk Hallam to manage some acres rented from Newdigate.

Evans's duties at the Arbury estate included acting as a relief officer. He distributed assistance to the poor and helped administer the workhouse, the hospital trust, and the Sunday school. He called Newdigate's attention to the need to lower rents when the harvest was poor. Mary Anne acquired from him a sympathy and sense of responsibility for the welfare of working families; she saw how they went hungry when the crops were bad and how their children suffered when their shoes were worn through.

⟨⟨    ⟩⟩

MANY would later remark on the absence of significant mothers in the fiction of George Eliot. The well-chronicled depressions in Mary Anne Evans's life may have stemmed from the fact that her mother did not love her—not in the way that a child needs for self-confidence throughout life. In Mary Anne's personal journals and diaries there is little evidence that her own mother figured very strongly in her life except to register disapproval. Her mother was aggravated by Mary Anne's straight and wispy hair, which resisted all efforts to keep it out of her eyes—so unlike her elder sister Chrissey's hair, blonde and curly, as a girl's should be.[1] Her brother later recalled that he had been his mother's favorite, and that Chrissey was the favorite of their aunts because she, unlike Mary Anne, was always neat and tidy. Fortunately for the little girl, she became her father's pet. Clever and interested in everything he did, she was a good companion for Evans, who was then in his mid-forties. He took his "little wench," as he called her, with him as he drove on his rounds. It was he who gave her her first book, *The Linnet's Life*. She loved the pictures, especially one showing the linnet (a common gray-brown songbird) feeding her young.

Mary Anne would accompany her father along the mile-long drive leading up to Arbury Hall, an Elizabethan mansion romanticized in the eighteenth century with Gothic revival touches such as battlements, fan-vaulting, turrets, and oriel windows. While Evans transacted his business, his daughter would sit obediently with the housekeeper or servants in an anteroom. She did the same when he went to nearby Astley Castle to see his employer's son, Colonel Newdigate. At her father's side, Mary Anne absorbed the rhythms of the agricultural year. All her life the sight of well-kept fields would please her; she would always prefer country to town. She also accepted as the natural order of things the stratification of a community by property and rank and later wove it lovingly into the background of her best novels set in England.

Very bright yet unsure of herself, Mary Anne doted on her brother Isaac, who was about three years older. Isaac was the center of her life. Together they spent part of each day at a dame school (a small informal school run by a local housewife) across from Griff. The rest of the day she followed him like a puppy and watched him fish. Some biographers have assumed that Mary Anne expressed the strength of this early attachment in an emotional passage cut out from a draft of *The Mill on the Floss*. Movingly, it describes how little Maggie Tulliver adores her older brother Tom,

> who liked no one to play with him but Maggie; they went out together somewhere every day, and carried either hot buttered cakes with them because it was baking day, or apple-puffs well sugared; Tom was never angry with her for forgetting things, and liked her to tell him tales....Above all, Tom loved her—oh, so much,—more even than she loved him, so that he would always want to have her with him and be afraid of vexing her; and he as well as every one else, thought her very clever.

Their closeness was shaken when, at the age of eight, Isaac was sent away to school at Foleshill, on the outskirts of Coventry. Losing her closest companion was painful enough, but when Isaac returned for the holidays, it seemed to Mary Anne he had changed. The gulf between them widened when he was given a pony and was free to roam by himself. Many forces converge to pull an older sibling away from an adoring younger one, but Mary Anne never stopped loving the brother whom, even then, she felt she had lost.

Christiana Evans seemed to prefer a child-free household. The two children from her husband's first marriage were packed off early—Robert, at seventeen, was sent to run the Kirk Hallam holdings in Derbyshire, and with him, his young sister Fanny, to keep house. In 1824, at age five, Mary Anne herself was sent away to join Chrissey as a boarder at Miss Lathom's school in Attleborough, less than a mile from Griff.

At Miss Lathom's she presented an odd combination of intelligence and awkwardness. She could not push past the older girls to get near the fire. Her suffering from the cold was an early sign of the poor health that was to cloud her life. She became afraid of the dark and suffered from night terrors. Frequently she burst into tears. One of her schoolmates remembered her as "a queer, three-cornered, awkward girl, who sat in corners and shyly watched her elders."

As a young child, she had been slow to learn to read; her half-sister, Fanny, assumed it was because she preferred to play outdoors with Isaac. However, by the age of seven, she had plunged into *Waverley*, by Sir Walter Scott, and was inconsolable when the book had to be returned to a neighbor before she had finished it. Out of frustration she began to write out an end to the story herself.

In 1828, when she was eight, Mary Anne was moved to Mrs. Wallington's, one of the best boarding schools in Nuneaton. It cost more than Miss Lathom's, but her parents did not balk at the expense of sending both their girls to a school that would smooth the rough edges of an agricultural childhood, teaching them manners, the piano, and French. It was considered an investment to prepare their daughters either to find good husbands or to support themselves as governesses. As the school was not far from home, the girls returned to Griff at weekends. During the week their father would drop by to see how they were getting along. He also saw to it that they got fresh eggs and country produce at the school.

There were thirty girls, all boarders, at Mrs. Wallington's. The school was run by three Irishwomen: Mrs. Wallington, from Cork, her eldest daughter Nancy, and Miss Maria Lewis. When her father fetched Mary Anne home for her tenth birthday, Miss Lewis came with them, and they all went to Chilvers Coton parish church together. The Evans family now recognized that Mary Anne was unusually clever and watched with pleasure the charades that she and Isaac would act out to entertain the household and visiting aunts.

In Miss Lewis, Mary Anne found the first person to perceive her intellectual gifts and also someone to provide the sympathetic mother figure she craved. She shared two characteristics with this favorite teacher: intellectual curiosity and a conspicuous lack of beauty. Miss Lewis had a severe squint that effectively doomed her to spinsterhood.

But Miss Lewis was more than a teacher. She was an evangelist, a disciple of the charismatic preacher John Edmund Jones, who was, like John Wesley, a Church of England evangelical. The challenge of Wesley's Methodism, as well as the vitality of Dissenting sects such as the Baptists, Presbyterians, and Congregationalists, had forced the Anglican Church to make a corner for evangelists, for whom ritual, liturgy, and the sacrament were less important than prayer and a knowledge of the Bible. Instead, they emphasized spreading the good tidings of the Gospels and striving for salvation through introspection and self-deprecation. Against this background, Miss Lewis guided her eager pupil into intensive Bible reading.

In Nuneaton, Jones's passionate sermons caused great division. Someone once threw a rock at him through the church window; his life was under constant threat. Robert Evans himself was moved to join the throng who went to hear the sermons, although he himself never veered from the High Anglican path favored by Arbury Hall. (However, his brother Samuel had become a Methodist, and Elizabeth, Samuel's wife, a Methodist preacher.)

Mary Anne's personal combination of strong intellect, wide reading, and low self-esteem made her vulnerable to a doctrine of self-effacement and duty toward others. She also acquired a lifelong interest in the dilemmas of clergymen struggling to be true to faith and flock. Clerics would be among the most vivid characters in her fiction.

Later, she and Maria Lewis would keep up an extensive correspondence (in which Mary Anne would sign herself Polly—a nickname for Mary). In those letters, as well as in her reading, Mary Anne reveals an interest in philosophy and ethics extraordinary in a young girl. As Eliot biographer Kathryn Hughes wrote in *George Eliot: The Last Victorian,* "If loving God was what it took to keep Miss Lewis loving her, Mary Anne was happy to oblige."

Mary Anne's devotion to God and to her teacher would carry her through the next decade.

## Chapter Two

# A SAINT, PERHAPS? (1832–1841)

WHEN MARY ANNE was twelve, she moved to the best girls' school in the Midlands. It was run by the Franklin sisters, daughters of a Coventry Baptist minister and themselves fervent evangelists, well read and well spoken. One had studied in Paris, where she acquired fluent French. This step up in scholastic rigor gave Mary Anne her first taste of a wider world; one pupil was from New York, another from India. Her sister Chrissey did not make the move—the school was too academic for her. After finishing at Mrs. Wallington's school in Nuneaton, Chrissey returned home to Griff, while Mary Anne remained with the Franklins until she was sixteen.

Franklin girls were urged to read widely. Mary Anne's taste was extended beyond the Bible to Shakespeare, Milton, Pope, Byron, and Wordsworth. Maria Lewis sent her a novel; in response, Mary Anne sent back a surprisingly self-analytical confession about the temptations of fiction as a refuge from reality: "When I was quite a little child I could not be satisfied with the things around me; I was constantly living in a world of my own creation, and was quite contented to have no companions that I might be left to my own musings and imagine scenes in which I was chief actress."

From the start, Mary Anne's work was outstanding. In her first year she won the French prize (a copy of Pascal's *Pensées*) and she began to append to her notebooks a Frenchified version of her name, Marianne Evans. Her teachers read her essays for pleasure. One of her papers, which was remarkably confident and didactic for a girl of fourteen, was titled "Admiration and Conceit." In strong language, she condemned affectation as "one of the most contemptible weaknesses of the human species." Conceited men, she went on, were guilty of the "deceit of affectation" while women "who set great store by their personal charms" seemed concerned not only to elicit the admiration of one sex but at the same time "the envy of the other."[1]

This pedagogic essay, with its psychological probing into human motives, suggests that she was both steeling herself against envying prettier girls, and preparing the moral groundwork to tell others how to live.

At the Franklins' school, Mary Anne worked very hard. Already she was an accomplished pianist, and the school often invited her to play for visitors. But her fine performances were often marred because she would end up running off in tears, convinced she had done badly. She worked on her speech, too. With diligence and deliberation, she eradicated her Midlands accent and the halting phrases of a farm girl. She lowered and modulated her voice; for the rest of her life the low, musical quality of her speech would be one of her most distinctive characteristics.

Even so, she retained a good ear for the local dialect. In a letter to a friend many years later, she spelled out how to speak it: "self" was "sen," "year" was " 'ear," and "head" "yead." In "of," the *f* was never pronounced, nor the *n* in "in."

At the Franklins' school, Mary Anne also displayed religious zeal. She would burst into spontaneous prayer and invite her schoolmates to join her; in response, they regarded her not with ridicule but with awe. The older girls made a pet of her and used to call her "little mamma."

On Sundays, she and her schoolmates attended the Cow Lane Baptist Chapel in Coventry to hear the Franklins' brother preach. He offered a liberal but self-castigating approach to faith and salvation. Taking on a new puritanical fervor, Mary Anne began to neglect her appearance in order to avoid vanity and self-indulgence.

A poem in her school notebook declares: "A Saint! Oh would that I could claim / The privileg'd, the honor'd name." The line suggests that she knows she is not as saintly as other people think.

The same notebook contains what is probably her first piece of historical fiction. Written at the age of fourteen, the fragment shows early signs of the realistic novelist she would become, as well as the influence of the novels of Walter Scott. She opens her story in Cromwellian England around 1650 with the mysterious young stranger who is attempting to find his uncle, who is imprisoned for life in Chepstow Castle for signing the death warrant of King Charles I, executed in 1649. The story peters out after several dozen pages, but the fragment shows that from the start Mary Anne loved recreating the past with eloquent and vivid descriptions of clothes and castles.

❦          ❧

IN addition to her literary interests, Mary Anne was also becoming alert to the challenge science presented to religious belief. Geology, then an emerging science, explained what was becoming apparent with the excavations for railway construction: that the layers of rocks and fossils uncovered could not have been created in six days, as the Bible claimed. Charles Lyell's *Principles of Geology*, published in three volumes between 1830 and 1833, was a popular success, running into many editions.

It was a time of dramatic political change as well. The Reform Act of 1832 partly corrected the system of government representation by redistributing parliamentary seats to correspond with large centers of population, such as Birmingham, which previously were unrepresented. The act abolished the "rotten" boroughs (those having fewer than two thousand inhabitants) and "pocket" boroughs (in which patrons personally chose two Members to represent the district) and also halved the number of MPs for towns of between two thousand and four thousand people. In urban districts, it gave the vote to all men who paid an annual rent of £10 or more for their houses. A property qualification was likewise set up for those living in the country.

A Conservative who opposed reform, Robert Evans once gave the estate's tenants a breakfast on election morning to induce them to vote Conservative. In practical terms, however, the

Whig party's reform did little to change the balance of power in Britain. The old principle prevailed: power was tied to land, and only those with a stake in property should have the right to vote. It enfranchised neither factory nor agricultural workers.

Just before Christmas 1832, Mary Anne witnessed violent riots at Nuneaton, stirred up by the first election after the Reform Act. At stake was the seat for North Warwickshire. Supporters of the new Radical candidate fought to keep those of the Conservative incumbent from reaching the polling place. Military force—a detachment of Scots Greys—was called in but could not calm the mob, and two soldiers were beaten and stripped naked. The Riot Act was read from the windows of the Newdigate Arms; Colonel Newdigate was personally injured and another man died. The ugly scene stayed with Mary Anne and later inspired her novel *Felix Holt: The Radical*.

At the same time, Robert Evans's own relation to the gentry was changing. In 1835, his longtime employer Francis Parker Newdigate died; Arbury Hall then passed not to Newdigate's son Francis, whom Evans knew well, but to his cousin's wife, Mrs. Newdigate, and her son Charles.

The new owners preferred the old spelling of the family name, Newdegate; Charles, later Member of Parliament for North Warwickshire, styled himself Newdigate Newdegate. Evans was then under their direction and for the rest of his life would be caught up in disputes between the rival sides of the family.

Returning home from school at Christmas in 1835, just after her sixteenth birthday, Mary Anne found her mother seriously ill with what appears to have been breast cancer. On New Year's Eve, Robert Evans also fell ill, with an intensely painful attack of kidney stones. He was treated with the medieval-era methods of the day—leeches and bloodletting—while his wife's life ebbed away in intense pain and paralysis. After a few days Mary Anne wrote to Maria Lewis that her father, at least, was out of danger. On February 3, 1836, Christiana Evans died. Chrissey, Isaac, and Mary Anne were at her bedside to watch the agonizing scene, recorded in Robert Evans's diary as "Dreadful night of pain."

There was no question of Mary Anne's returning to school following her mother's death. As the elder daughter, Chrissey became housekeeper; Isaac helped his father with the estate, and Mary Anne's duty was to help her sister. Yet she never stopped educating herself. The range and depth of her reading in history, biography, and theology as a teenager at Griff was extraordinary.

Although they were stuffy about their surname, the Newdegates were no snobs. Mrs. Charles Newdegate, now mistress of Arbury Hall, admired Mary Anne's work for the poor. Knowing the girl's appetite for books, she invited her to use the splendid library of the great house.

In the spring of 1837, Chrissey Evans did as her family expected and made what seemed to be a good match, marrying a surgeon, Edward Clarke. The younger son of the squire of Brooksby Hall near Leicester, Clarke served as medical officer to the workhouse administered by Robert Evans. Signing the register as bridesmaid, Mary Anne omitted for the first time the final *e* from her name—a sign, perhaps, of a new sense of maturity. Afterward, she and Isaac wept over the breakup of the family and the end of their childhood. It was to be their last close moment.

Isaac and Mary Anne were opposites in many aspects of their lives—he was High Church Anglican, modeling himself on the gentry; she was puritanical and evangelical. When Isaac took her on her first trip to London, in 1838, he was astonished that what impressed his sister most in their week of intensive sightseeing was the great bell of St. Paul's. However, she disdained the church's choir, just as she denied herself the frivolous pleasure of the theater, and spent all her evenings alone, reading. Isaac bought himself some hunting prints. The chief purchase she wanted to make in the capital was Josephus's *History of the Jews*. It was the first sign of a lifelong fascination with Judaism.

Mary Ann, as she now wrote her name, was also teaching herself Latin. Inspired by the Arbury Hall library, in 1839 she decided to compile a chart of ecclesiastical history, which correlated the dates of the Roman Empire with the writings, schisms, and heresies that marked the development of Christianity from the birth of Jesus to the Reformation. Not that she despised housework; following Chrissey's marriage, she was now in charge of running Griff House. She was a perfectionist. She helped her father choose a new sideboard and wallpaper for Griff. With Mrs. Newdegate, she distributed clothing and blankets to the poor on the estate and took responsibility for visiting forty-two families. She supervised the dairy and made currant jelly, damson cheese, and mince pies. She prepared celebrations and feasts for Isaac's birthday. Outside the home, however, she had next to no social life; she went to one dance, but all she got out of it was a headache—a symptom that would long plague her. She despaired of ever achieving anything in her own right.

She was a pious nineteen-year-old when Elizabeth Evans, wife of Robert Evans's brother Samuel, visited the family. A tiny woman with bright, small, dark eyes, Elizabeth had been a Methodist preacher; she gave up the role only when women were no longer allowed to preach. From her rich experience, she told her niece a harrowing story. She had visited a young woman in prison, condemned to death for murdering her newborn child. She assisted the prisoner—"a common coarse girl"—to a peaceful death by persuading her to ask God's forgiveness, then accompanied her to the gallows. It was the kind of first-person report that no one could forget, especially not when it was delivered in a strong Midlands accent by a woman who believed in miracles. Mary Ann stored the tale away along with her memories of the Nuneaton riots.

Robert Evans, for his part, was proud of his daughter and respected her abilities. From the local bookseller, he ordered all the heavy theological books she wanted. He found her a tutor for modern languages and another for music; he enjoyed hearing her play for him in the evenings. When she turned twenty, in November 1839, he took her to London, her first trip on a train. She stayed with a school friend, Jessie Barclay, for five days while he transacted estate business.

On her twentieth birthday she reported to Maria Lewis that the poetry of Wordsworth expressed many of her own feelings in just the way she wished—a hint that she was losing her evangelical fervor and shifting to Romantic ideas. As she told a school friend, Patty Jackson, she also voraciously read natural science "to make up for girlish miseducation and girlish idleness."

At the end of 1839, at Maria's suggestion, Mary Ann sent a poem about a lonely walk to the *Christian Observer*, which published it in January 1840. Signed M.A.E., the poem was her first appearance in print. The lines capture the depressive cast of the lonely artist, one to whom books "have been...as chests of gold" but who also hears a small voice telling her to say "Farewell!" to books, to earth, "and all that breathe earth's air."

From the spring of 1840, a new tutor, Joseph Brezzi, came to teach her German and Italian. Like many vulnerable girls, she fell hopelessly in love with her teacher. She found him, she told Patty, "anything but uninteresting, all external grace and mental power." Brezzi was the first in a long line of disappointing crushes that convinced her she was unlovable.

Around this time, she wrote to Maria Lewis that she saw herself as "involuntarily isolated." She sounded even more forlorn in a letter she wrote to Patty Jackson: "Every day's experience seems to deepen the voice of foreboding that has long been telling me, 'The bliss of reciprocated affection is not allotted to you under any form.'"

Her meaning could not be clearer. As she approached twenty-one, well read and reading more, Mary Ann Evans was preparing herself for a life alone.

# Chapter Three

# COVENTRY AWAKENING (1841–1849)

I N March 1841, Robert Evans retired from land management and made the move from country to city in order to place Mary Ann in a wider social circle where she might find a husband. Otherwise, who would support her when he died? Isaac was the only apparent alternative, and neither he nor his fiancée welcomed the prospect. (Isaac married Sarah Rawlins, who was ten years his senior, in June 1841, and they planned to live at Griff.)

The move to the outskirts of Coventry had a transforming effect on the twenty-one-year-old Mary Ann. Coventry, the home of Lady Godiva, had stood at the crossroads of medieval England and by the mid-nineteenth century was the industrial hub of the Midlands. In Coventry, after initial months of loneliness, Mary Ann encountered a new world, far wider than anything she had glimpsed as a boarder at the Franklins' school. She met sophisticated people who were as unconventional in their morals as they were in their theology. Neither evangelicals nor Anglicans, they were freethinkers who boldly questioned the existence of God and the veracity of the Bible.

The Evanses' new house, Bird Grove, lay in a district called Foleshill. Mary Ann struck up a friendship with her new neighbors, Abijah and Elizabeth Pears, who were both from families prominent in the important local ribbon-weaving industry. They entertained friends with musical evenings at which Mary Ann played the piano.

Through the Pearses she met Cara Bray, Elizabeth's sister, and her husband Charles—the couple who would change her life. The Brays lived within walking distance in an impressive home, with gables and spacious grounds, called Rosehill. The Brays were intellectuals and progressives. Charles Bray was eight years older than Mary Ann and probably the handsomest man she had ever seen. With his knowing eyes and broad, sensual lips, he was rumored to be "the Don Juan of Coventry." His many affairs were believed to have included his wife's older sister, Mary Hennell. He was understood also to have encouraged his wife to have an affair with a man with whom he knew she was in love, Edward Noel.

There was another Hennell sister, Sara, who was older and more widely read than Cara. She lived in London but was often at Rosehill and soon became Mary Ann's closest friend. Handsome and well-read, Sara had spent many years as governess to distinguished families. She was as musical as Mary Ann, and the two sang duets. She was also well-read in philosophy and theology. Before long, Sara Hennell had displaced the devout Maria Lewis as Mary Ann's trusted confidante and become her partner in an erudite and frequently impassioned correspondence that lasted until Mary Ann's death.

Sara dubbed Mary Ann "Pollian"—a play on the nickname Polly and on Apollyon, the Angel of Destruction in the New Testament's Book of Revelation. Charles Bray, for his part, was struck by Mary Ann's intelligence and stimulating conversation. While he noticed her depression, he found her a delightful companion—unaggressive, superbly read, and full of social conscience. She was appalled, as she had told Maria Lewis, by "the prevalence of misery and want in this boasted nation of prosperity and glory."

Bray had inherited a lucrative ribbon business from his father in 1835 and used his independence to advance his Radical, agnostic, and social-reform ideas. Strongly concerned for the welfare of the poor, he started a cooperative store to undercut other shops and give customers a share in the profits. He also launched the Working Men's Club, which did not allow its members to drink alcohol, and opened a school for young children in a poor neighborhood.

Rosehill, with its countrylike setting, was the center of Coventry's intelligentsia. "I do indeed feel that I shut the world out when I shut that door," Mary Ann told Mary Sibree, another congenial neighbor. For Mary Ann, Rosehill was the university that she never would attend (women were at that time forbidden to attend English universities). In this libertarian atmosphere, divorce, population control, and sexual education were among the subjects discussed in mixed company. Very soon, Mary Ann had adopted a new view of marriage, declaring "the truth of feeling as the only universal bond of union."

Charles Bray may have been enlightened on the principle of contraception, but not its practice. While Cara seemed infertile, Bray's mistress, the cook at Rosehill, bore him six children, one of whom, a little daughter, was brought into the household as his and Cara's "adopted" child. Few couples knew how to limit their families at the time. Mary Ann's sister Chrissey Clarke, living in Meriden, west of Coventry, already had four children and would go on to produce two more. Her husband, Edward Clarke, who considered himself a modern medical man, was no more inclined to practice birth control than was Charles Bray.[1]

In this stimulating and skeptical atmosphere, Mary Ann's adolescent puritanism fell away fast. She was astonished and delighted to learn that Cara Bray's brother was the author Charles Hennell, who had written *An Inquiry Concerning the Origin of Christianity*. The book, a remarkable examination of the historical origins of Jesus Christ and the Bible, had caused a stir when it was published, in 1838. For Mary Ann, who had done her own research on ecclesiastical history, Hennell's bold inquiry was just what she wanted to read.

In fact, it was only a matter of months after moving to Coventry before Miss Evans lost her faith altogether. By November 1841, as she reached twenty-two, she faced the practical question, How could she celebrate the religious festival of Christmas? However, she decided to keep her thoughts to herself and attend church as she was expected to do—all the more because she had been feeling lonely and had invited Maria Lewis to stay at Bird Grove over the holiday.

However, the atmosphere turned sour at Christmas dinner. Around the table were her father; Chrissey and her husband, Edward Clarke; Mary Ann's brother Isaac and his wife, Sarah; her half-sister Fanny Houghton and her husband, Henry; and Maria. They fell into an acrimonious discussion of Mary Ann's worrying friendship with the Brays. Isaac's fear (as he told his father) was that Mary Ann had no chance of finding a husband if she mixed only with known Chartists and Radicals.

The confrontation made Mary Ann feel that she should be true to her own conscience. As she entered 1842, she inscribed her copy of the second edition of Hennell's book "Mary Ann Evans. January 1st 1842," as though to affirm her New Year's resolution to come out into the open as a nonbeliever. The following day, a Sunday, she refused to go to church. For her father, who was a pillar of Holy Trinity Church, her announcement meant public humiliation. He knew that his daughter's absence would be recognized for what it was: defiance. For several Sundays, Mary Ann persisted in staying at home, while her father and Isaac grew angrier. She stated her case in a long, reasoned letter to her father, declaring that it would be hypocritical to join in a worship in which she did not believe. At the same time, she reassured him she was not going to join any other Christian community, such as the Unitarians.

*While I admire and cherish much of what I believe to have been the moral teaching of Jesus himself, I consider that the system of doctrines built upon the facts of his life and drawn as to its materials from Jewish notions to be most dishonourable to God and most pernicious in its influence on individual and social happiness.... Such*

*being my very strong convictions, it cannot be a question with any*
*mind of strict integrity, whatever judgement may be passed on their*
*truth, that I could not without vile hypocrisy and a miserable truck-*
*ling to the smile of the world for the sake of my supposed interests,*
*profess to join in worship which I wholly disapprove.*

Isaac and Chrissey began a determined campaign to reason her
back into a belief in religion and life after death. They enlisted
friends such as Maria Lewis, Mary Sibree, and Mrs. Pears, as
well as several clergymen. One, the Reverend Francis Watts, a
married professor of theology at Birmingham, found himself so
engaged and enchanted by this young woman that he entered a
translation project with her.

All their efforts were to no avail. Mary Ann would not recant.
The move to Coventry now seemed a wasted expense, having been
made, as Mary Ann had commented sarcastically in her long letter to her father, with "no other object than to give me a centre in
society." Robert Evans angrily put their house on the market.

For her part, Mary Ann claimed she would as happily live
with him and look after him at the cottage given to him by Lord
Aylesford, for whom he was then agent, in the nearby village of
Packington.

To escape the tension at home, she went briefly to Chrissey's,
but when Chrissey became ill, Mary Ann took two of her neph-
ews with her and returned to her father's house. This was her
first discovery that she was good at mothering boys, which she
would have much more experience with later in life.

The next step in her life, Cara Bray suggested, should be
teaching, but Mary Ann would not consider it. She went back

to Nuneaton to live at Griff with Isaac and his wife for nearly a month. They were kind to her and persuaded her that concili-ation was the wisest course of action: she would resume going to church with her father and keep her thoughts to herself. The Brays and her former schoolmistress Rebecca Franklin agreed. Robert Evans accepted the compromise; he had missed his daughter more than he acknowledged, and they resumed living together at Bird Grove. Their "holy war" had come to an end.

Mary Ann's infatuation with Charles Bray intensified during the ensuing year, 1842, when they were often seen walking arm in arm. Yet she was so plain that Cara Bray was not jealous. To the Brays, the prodigiously well-read Mary Ann was not a threat but an acquisition. Cara and Sara wondered whether perhaps their brother Charles Hennell, whom Mary Ann had met and found "a perfect model of manly excellence," might suit her.

Sadly, Hennell was already engaged. When his startling book first came out, he had been invited to Wiltshire by a rational-ist admirer, Dr. Robert Brabant, who was working on a book (which he never finished) dismissing the supernatural elements in religion. Brabant had a beautiful daughter with red-gold hair named Elizabeth but known as Rufa. Not only was she lovely to look at, but like her father she was a scholar, interested in philosophy and theology. At Hennell's suggestion, she began translating D. F. Strauss's *Das Leben Jesu*, published in German in 1835—a three-volume critical examination of the life of Jesus that denied the historical value of the Gospels. Within a week of meeting her, Hennell had proposed. However, Brabant forbade the marriage on the grounds that Hennell was consumptive, or at least had a family history of tuberculosis. It was a perfect match, however, and the romance continued nonetheless, sustained through their mutual work on translation.

When Hennell introduced Rufa to Mary Ann at Rosehill, Mary Ann did not like her at first, but the two women warmed to each other as they discussed German theology. (Two years earlier, working with Brezzi, Mary Ann had decided that she had a greater affinity with German than Italian.) Mary Ann later explained to Sara Hennell that her initial reaction was "unfavourable and unjust for in spite of what some caustic people say, I fall not in love with every one."

In May 1843, Charles Hennell was invited to join the party when Mary Ann, with her father's permission, traveled with Sara and the Brays to Stratford-upon-Avon, Malvern, and Tenby. On the Welsh coast at Tenby, the Brays' dreams of making a match between Hennell and Mary Ann Evans were finally dashed. Rufa Brabant joined them and renewed her engagement to Hennell. Dr. Brabant gave in and allowed the marriage to go ahead despite his concerns about Hennell's weak chest. (Brabant's suspicions were well founded; Hennell died of tuberculosis less than eight years later.)

Rufa took an interest in Mary Ann, and at Tenby, perhaps intending it as a consolation, persuaded her to go to a ball. But whatever good intentions she may have had were thwarted; Mary Ann's evening ended in humiliation because no one asked her to dance. In November, Rufa invited her to be bridesmaid, and Mary Ann accepted. The wedding took place in London, at the Unitarian Chapel in Finsbury. Mary Ann would make her third visit to London for the occasion; this time she stayed with Sara Hennell at her home in Hackney.

At the wedding, Rufa's father, a small, flirtatious sixty-two-year-old, had invited Mary Ann to accompany him home for a holiday, and a few weeks later, Mary Ann went to stay with him in Wiltshire. Brabant seemed intent on replacing his "lost" daughter with her bridesmaid. It was too easily done. Mary Ann proceeded to fall in love with him—or so it seemed to his family, who watched the pedantic couple walking arm in arm, reading German aloud, engrossed in each other. Mary Ann wrote to Cara Bray that she was "in a little heaven here Dr. Brabant being its archangel." Indeed, she seems to have been ready to accept Brabant's suggestion that she join the household, and wrote to her father asking to stay two weeks longer. That was not to be.

Dr. Brabant's wife was blind, but not so blind as to ignore what her sister was telling her—that her husband and his visitor were enraptured with each other. The two women ordered Mary Ann out. Mrs. Brabant told Mary Ann that if she did not leave the house, she herself would. Worse, Brabant ungallantly pretended it was Mary Ann's fault. She was back in Coventry ten days before she had hoped. Nothing is known about the physical relations between the doctor and his guest, but Brabant (along with Charles Bray) remains a contender as the man who took Mary Ann's virginity.

After this episode, Mary Ann was still at a loss about what to do with her life. Judging by a letter written on March 30 by Cara to her sister Sara—the only evidence of this tantalizing episode—in 1845, Mary Ann became briefly engaged to a young artist who worked as a picture restorer at a stately home at Baginton, two miles south of Griff. Without giving his name,

Cara informed her sister:

> *Well, they did meet and passed two days in each other's company,*
> *and she thought him the most interesting young man she had seen*
> *and superior to all the men of mankind; the third morning he made*
> *proposals through her brother in law Mr. Hooton [Houghton]—*
> *saying, "she was the most fascinating creature he had ever beheld,*
> *that if it were not too presumptuous to hope etc. etc., a person of*
> *such superior excellence and powers of mind," etc., in short, he*
> *seemed desperately smitten and begged permission to write to her.*
> *She granted this, and came to us so brimful of happiness;—though*
> *she said she had not fallen in love with him yet, but admired his*
> *character so much that she was sure she should: the only objections*
> *seem to be that his profession—a picture-restorer—is not lucrative*
> *or over-honourable.*

Cara continued, writing that when the young man had come
to visit Mary Ann, he "did not seem to her half so interesting as before, and the next day she made up her mind that she
could never love or respect him enough to marry him and that it
would involve too great a sacrifice of her mind and pursuits."

With much anxiety, Mary Ann wrote her young man a letter,
turning him down. Both sisters thought she had made a mistake. Mary Ann herself was racked with headaches, unsure that
she had done the right thing.

She was determined as well not to be rushed (as she felt Cara
Bray had been) into a hasty marriage she would spend the rest of
her life regretting. At that time in England there was no possibility of divorce except on grounds of adultery or madness, a pro-
cedure requiring a costly petition to Parliament. Beginning in

January 1844, Mary Ann found the perfect outlet for her intellectual energies: she took over the translation of Strauss's fifteen-hundred-page *Das Leben Jesu*, which Rufa had abandoned when she married Hennell. At first, Sara had taken over but then gave up, and Mary Ann was looking for a new translation project. Earlier, she had asked the theologian Francis Watts, with whom she had corresponded over her religious doubts, to oversee her translation of a philosophical work that much appealed to her. Written in French by the Swiss theologian Alexandre Vinet, *Mémoire en faveur de la liberté des cultes* defended man's innate conscience and capacity for goodness. But that project had ended in embarrassment, as Mary Ann assumed that Watts's interest in her was personal rather than intellectual:

> *A friend has given some admonitions that led me to fear I have misrepresented myself by my manner. . . . It gives me much pain to think that you should have received such an impression, and I entreat you to believe that the remembrance of you, your words and looks calls up, I will not say humble, but self-depreciating reflections and lively gratitude.*

Taking up *Das Leben Jesu*, Mary Ann was soon translating six pages a day. She was well equipped; her German was excellent, and she was a skeptical humanist, eager for a rationalist attack on the Bible. She was aware of the low status of women, and her self-esteem as a writer could hardly have been lower. She was appalled when she heard that someone had told Strauss that "a young lady" was translating his book. She wrote that "he must have some twinges of alarm to think he was dependent on that most contemptible specimen of the human being for his English reputation." But she got the job done, and it was her first published book. *The Life of Jesus, Critically Examined by David Friedrich Strauss*, translated from the fourth German edition, was brought out in three volumes by John Chapman, Newdigate Street, London, on June 15, 1846. The book, with its reasoned skepticism, had a deep influence on the religious debates of mid-Victorian England. Its publication was subsidized by the Radical Member of Parliament Joseph Parkes, who paid £300, £20 of which was paid to the unnamed translator, who had worked on the book for two years.

In the spring of 1845, the Brays introduced Mary Ann to a distant relative, the well-known writer and social reformer Harriet Martineau. Martineau, then in her forties, was the first Englishwoman to become an influential writer on politics and society. She opposed slavery and argued for trade unionism and women's education. She was also in favor of mesmerism, which she believed had cured her of a painful gynecological ailment. It had not, however, cured the deafness that forced her to carry a large ear trumpet. But for Mary Ann, Martineau, with her prodigious output of articles, pamphlets, novels, and biographies, was an inspiring example of what a scholarly Englishwoman, like herself, could achieve through her own abilities, provided she did as Harriet Martineau had done: got out of the provinces, established herself in London, and threw herself into her work.

In October 1845, with the Strauss book sent to the printer, Mary Ann planned to go to the Scottish Highlands with "her dear trio"—the Brays and Sara Hennell. Robert Evans at first tried to put a stop to it; he hadn't forgiven the Brays for converting his daughter to agnosticism. But Charles Bray pleaded that she needed a change of scene and he relented. In Scotland, the landscape of Sir Walter Scott's novels, Mary Ann fell into raptures. But the trip was cut short by a summons from home: her father had broken his leg and needed her immediately. It was the beginning of several years of illness and steady decline, during which he came to depend on his daughter as never before.

In June 1846, Charles Bray bought the *Coventry Herald and Observer* (to give it its full name) as a vehicle for his ideas on social reform and invited Mary Ann to become his assistant. He asked her to write book reviews for the newspaper as well as witty articles. (These would be anonymous, according to the conventions of the time.) This she did for three years. It was her way into journalism, the chance to see her words in print regularly—not only reviews but her own original thoughts and satiric commentary. She wrote five sketches that appeared in the *Herald* between December 1846 and February 1847 under the heading "Poetry and Prose from the Notebook of an Eccentric" and revealed a gift for social commentary and ironic prose.

When Mary Ann's translation of Strauss's *Das Leben Jesu*, with its apparent attack on religion, came out in July 1846, what remained of her friendship with Maria Lewis was severed. In 1846, just before her book came out, Mary Ann made another trip to London, again staying with Sara. She met her publisher Chapman, who she immediately saw was dangerously attractive. He was one of the handsomest men of his time: six feet tall, with high cheekbones, sparkling brown eyes, luxuriant hair, and a belief that love did not require the anointment of marriage. The journalist T. P. O'Connor, describing Chapman as an old man, wrote "even then he was beautiful." When Mary Ann met him, he was twenty-nine, with a well-to-do, pregnant wife of forty-three and three children.

Mary Ann, in contrast, was now approaching twenty-seven and was very conscious that she had no prospect of marriage and that the focus of her life would be intellectual. She tried to laugh off her predicament. In October, she composed a playful letter to Charles Bray about an imaginary admirer who allegedly had come to call on her, presenting his card as "Professor Bücherwurm." What the professor wanted, she said, was to find a wife who was a translator but who should also have "a very decided ugliness of person." Mary Ann told Bray she replied to the imaginary professor that she needed "nothing more in a husband than to save me from the horrific disgrace of spinsterhood and to take me out of England."

In the autumn of 1847 and the late spring of 1848, Mary Ann made trips with her father—first to the Isle of Wight, then to St. Leonards in Sussex (the first purpose-built seaside resort in Britain)—in an attempt to restore his health. She read to him the highly successful *Jane Eyre*, published in 1847 by Charlotte Brontë, under the pseudonym Currer Bell. She wrote to Charles Bray that "All self-sacrifice is good—but one would like it to be in a somewhat nobler cause than that of a diabolical law which chains a man soul and body to a putrefying carcase." By the following spring, Robert Evans was clearly dying. Mary Ann was constantly at his bedside. As relief from nursing, she threw herself into translating Benedict de Spinoza's *Tractatus Theologico-Politicus*, published in 1670, from Latin. She allowed herself to complain only to Sara: "My life is a perpetual nightmare, and always haunted by something to be done, which I have never the time, or rather the energy, to do." She had sat down in desperation that evening, only to find that "dear father is very uneasy, and his moans distract me."

Chapman had tentatively agreed to publish her Spinoza translation. Mary Ann was delighted, but she would struggle not to be smitten with this handsome publisher as she had been with Charles Bray. As she worked, she wrote to Sara that she was wary of Chapman: "he was always too much of the interesting gentleman to please me."

Meanwhile, another "interesting gentleman" presented himself: J. A. Froude, who had written a controversial novel called *The Nemesis of Faith*, a tale of a Church of England clergyman who falls into an adulterous love affair with the wife of a friend and loses his faith. The novel was denounced and a copy burned at Froude's Oxford college, Exeter, whereupon he resigned. It was just what the apostate Mary Ann wanted to read. She got the book, addressed to "the translator of Strauss," through Chapman. Mary Ann reviewed it rapturously in the *Coventry Herald* on March 16, 1849, calling it one of the rare books that suggest the necessity of reform in Christianity and "the true product of genius." She also wrote Froude a thank-you letter, keeping the pseudonym "the translator of Strauss."

Although Chapman would not divulge her name to Froude, he seems to have conveyed to him that the translator was female, for Froude wrote a charming request for a meeting; if he were indeed a fallen star, as the review had put it, perhaps she could help him to rise. The letter sent Mary Ann running giddily to Rosehill. Cara relayed to her sister Sara: "Poor girl! I am so pleased she should have this little episode in her dull life."

Before long, Froude was a guest at Rosehill, and Mary Ann went over to meet him. As Charles Bray watched the pair engage in lively discussion of the finer points of theology and Froude's book, his thoughts turned again to making a match. He invited Froude to join a party he was forming to travel to Geneva.

One physical feature of Mary Ann had particularly attracted Charles Bray: her large, bony skull. He was a believer in phrenology, the Victorian pseudoscience of judging human personality by the contours of the head. Bray examined the heads of everyone at Rosehill. He described Mary Ann's as showing a balance of "the Animal and Moral regions," with her intellect and moral feelings keeping her "animal" feelings in check.

The chief proponent of phrenology was George Combe, of Edinburgh. His *Outlines of Phrenology* had been a best seller in 1836. His beliefs were drawn, perhaps, from his own discordant conjunction of a large, handsome head atop a small, deformed body. He had his head shaved, the better to have its contours analyzed. In July 1848, Charles Bray brought Mary Ann to Combe in London to have a cast made of her skull. Combe allowed her to keep her hair, and the cast became a treasured keepsake in later years, when she had become more than an interesting neighbor of the Brays.

One glance told Combe that "Miss Evans's head is a very large one." He went on to describe her in weightier terms than Bray's: "the Intellect greatly predominates. . . . In the Feelings, the Animal and Moral regions are about equal; the moral being quite sufficient to keep the animal in order. . . . She was of a most affectionate disposition, always requiring some one to lean upon, preferring what has hitherto been considered the stronger sex, to the other and more impressible. She was not fitted to stand alone."

The observations were irrationally derived but psychologically accurate. The brilliant Mary Ann had her desires in check but had a constant need to be loved, and, as those close to her remarked, she needed a man at her side.

Looking at Bray's head, Combe delivered a stern prescription: Bray should, by diet, exercise, and every means available, strive "to lessen the vigor of his amativeness and be faithful to his wife." It was advice wasted.

TRANSLATING Spinoza helped Mary Ann through the long months of what she knew was her father's last illness. She read to him constantly and with loving patience. On May 10, 1849, she wrote to her neighbor Mrs. Pears that "his mind is as clear and rational as ever…and he gives me a thousand little proofs that he understands my affection and responds to it."

Robert Evans died on May 31, 1849. To Charles Bray, Mary Ann declared that her father "was the one strong deep love I have ever known…What shall I be without my Father?" She had never been happier than when she was nursing him through his last days, perhaps because she was relieved from the guilt about work undone. Her father had been her anchor. She felt as if "a part of my moral nature had gone." Without him, she feared that she might become "earthly sensual and devilish."

So she would. But not for a few years yet.

## Chapter Four

# HERSELF ALONE
# (1849–1851)

T HE BRAYS THOUGHT they could help Mary Ann recover from her father's death by taking her with them on their planned trip to Europe. On June 12, 1849, less than a week after the funeral, they swept her across the Channel. It was too soon. She was numb with grief. Even so, she was far better off than many unmarried women, who were often left destitute. The £100 in cash from her father's will gave her some freedom for the immediate future, in which she would have to find a new home for herself. She had also inherited £2,000 capital, as did her sister and half-sister, though both their shares had been absorbed by their dowries when they married; Chrissey's husband had already dissipated hers. But for Mary Ann the interest from the capital would yield her an annual income of £90, paid in semiannual installments by her brother. Thus she was modestly independent and could travel without financial concern.

The Brays had hoped to take Mary Ann's latest crush—J. A. Froude—with them to Europe, and he had agreed to go. Days before the departure, however, as the Brays and Mary Ann were in London preparing to take the train to Folkestone, John Chapman appeared with a note saying the last thing Mary Ann needed to hear: Froude could not travel because he was engaged to be married. Had Froude panicked at the thought of being paired for several weeks with the plain, intellectual Mary Ann Evans? We cannot know for certain but, in any event, he married soon after.

On the journey, which took them from Avignon via Nice to Genoa, Mary Ann was a listless, querulous traveling companion. The Brays finally decided to settle her in Geneva, where they found an agreeable pension for her out along the lake. She had once dreamed of spending some quiet months by herself in Geneva. Now that she was there, she found that she very much enjoyed exploring the city and meeting new people, although she felt conspicuous because she was alone. Her only friends were other tourists, and she spent much time in her room.

She had enough money to see her through until the end of the year if she lived frugally. From the money left in trust, however, she felt obliged to help out her sister; Chrissey's seven-year-old daughter had died recently of scarlet fever, and her short-sighted husband could hardly support their remaining children.

In October, as the cold swept in, Mary Ann moved to a more congenial pension in the center of Geneva. It was the home of a painter, François D'Albert-Durade, and his wife, Julie. Her host, then forty-five, was small, with a hunched back but an agreeable face that to her suggested artistic sensibility. D'Albert was fascinated by this phenomenally well-read young Englishwoman. She quickly came to look up to him as a mentor. She took his guidance to such an extent that she attended lectures in experimental physics twice a week at the University of Geneva. She also took "a dose of Mathematics every day to prevent my brain from getting soft."

Once more Mary Ann found herself enthralled by an older man. She had an ability that women once were urged to cultivate: to make a man feel wise and witty. The rapt attention of a woman as intelligent as Mary Ann was flattering to the male ego. Fortunately, D'Albert's wife, unlike Dr. Brabant's six years earlier, took a motherly interest in her husband's admirer. Indeed, Mary Ann was soon calling Madame D'Albert *Maman*. It was the first of many familial labels she would bestow on nonrelatives, as if in search of the family ties she had lost and the children she perhaps sensed that she would never have. She asked also, and received, Madame D'Albert's permission to address D'Albert in the familiar *tu* form.

D'Albert's own feelings may be judged by the portrait he painted of Mary Ann in November 1849, when she turned thirty. Perhaps the only flattering likeness ever done of her, the image is often used on the cover of her biographies. Painted in color, it minimizes her nose and chin and shows her full face with beautiful blue-gray eyes and a sweet smile.

The pretty portrait did little to change Mary Ann's view of herself. She laughed at the way a French marquise, one of the many international guests at her previous pension, had rearranged her hair. The marquise had abolished "all my curls and made two things stick out on each side of my head like those on the head of the Sphinx." Everyone at the time had told her she looked infinitely better, but she thought to herself that she looked "uglier than ever—if possible."

During the icy Swiss winter, Mary Ann considered her future. She decided she must return to England, but where to go? Neither Isaac nor Chrissey wanted her to live with them, and the feeling was mutual. She decided that she would like to make her way as a writer, as Harriet Martineau had done. In March 1850, in a fatherly gesture, D'Albert escorted her home, at his own expense, and stayed in England for some weeks. They traveled the first part of the way by sleigh, as the railway line was not yet open all the way to France. The Channel crossing was so rough that Mary Ann had to take to her bed in her London hotel immediately upon arrival, forcing her to miss an evening party at the home of her Strauss publisher, John Chapman. Had she gone to the party, she might have made important contacts, for she was weighing the possibility of moving to London and supplementing her income by writing articles for the serious reviews.[1]

In April, on a visit to her family in and around Nuneaton, she had such a cool reception that she wrote to Sara Hennell, "It was some envious demon that drove me across the Jura to come and see people who don't want me." She signed herself, as before, Pollian, but when writing to others, from the spring of 1851, she signed herself Marian. Escaping her family after a month, she returned to Coventry and lived at Rosehill for seven months, from May 1850 to January 1851. The Brays once more made her feel as if their spacious home was hers for as long as she wanted. They invited D'Albert for a visit, and she took him on a tour of the area, including Kenilworth Castle.

It was at Rosehill in October that Marian got to know her publisher, John Chapman. Marian was happy to get better acquainted with him; he had, after all, published the heretical Froude novel as well as her own Strauss translation. Traveling with Chapman was Robert Mackay, an author of a new book with the formidable title *The Progress of the Intellect as Exemplified in the Religious Development of the Greeks and the Hebrews*. Chapman saw immediately that Marian could be a great help to him in his publishing enterprises. Indeed, he was so impressed with her intellect and ability that he suggested she review Mackay's book for the *Westminster Review*, an eminent quarterly he was trying to buy.

Her achievement in composing a long, literate essay on the difficult book confirmed her determination to move to London and support herself by writing. In November 1850 she took the Mackay review to London by hand and, at Chapman's invitation, stayed at his home at 142 Strand, where there were a bookshop and publishing offices on the ground floor, while the family household and boarders occupied the four floors above. There she met his wife, Susanna, and his children's governess, Elisabeth Tilley, who was Chapman's mistress, although Marian did not know it at the time. She also got a taste of the brilliant literary parties for which 142 Strand was known. One evening she met Eliza Lynn, a published novelist whose success convinced her that she could write books, too. She returned to Coventry, determined to accept Chapman's offer to work for him.

In January 1851 she moved to London. Chapman met her at Euston Station and recorded in his diary that her manner was "friendly but formal and studied." He seems to have been aware that Elisabeth had written Marian two letters the previous week.[2]

In January, as she settled into 142 Strand, Marian's review of Mackay's *The Progress of the Intellect* appeared in the *Westminster Review*. As a working journalist, she was on her way.

Ten weeks later, however, she was on her way back to Coventry, forced out of London by the combined jealousy of Chapman's wife and his mistress, just as she had been expelled from Brabant's household in Wiltshire seven years earlier.

Chapman, it seems, had found her too interesting. He had spent hours in her room receiving lessons in German and listening to her play Mozart, until his wife felt compelled to buy a piano for the drawing room. He walked with Marian in St. James's and Hyde parks. Coded references in Chapman's diary suggest that their relationship went beyond merely strolling together.[3] Entries for January 19 and 20, 1851, seem to suggest there were two sexual encounters between him and Marian. One entry says "M. P.M.," the other "M. A.M." The same diary shows that Chapman liked keeping a sexual score. In the year that Marian Evans joined his household, he recorded on August 26, 1851, that he had had intercourse with Elisabeth Tilley for the fifty-third and fifty-fourth time that year. Later, when Marian became famous as George Eliot, Chapman deleted the January "M" entries, but not thoroughly enough to escape detection by the Yale scholars who later studied the diary.

These fragments bear out journalist T. P. O'Connor's recollection that, walking with Chapman past 142 Strand many years later, he mentioned that George Eliot had been in love with the writer Herbert Spencer. In reply, Chapman squeezed

O'Connor's arm and whispered, "You know, she was very fond of me!"

By March of that year, Chapman's wife and his mistress (who oddly seemed to show no jealousy of each other) had had enough. Tensions between the trio of women at 142 Strand began simmering on January 22, 1851 (two days after Chapman appears to have had sex with "M."), when he invited Marian to go for a walk. The other two women volunteered to come, too. Exasperated, Chapman said that all three could go without him. By February 18, wife and mistress declared they wanted Marian out. They had decided that she and Chapman were "completely in love with each other" after Susanna found her husband holding Marian's hand in her room. Chapman wrote in his diary that Susanna had told him never to go in her room again. (The threat did not keep Chapman from taking "Miss M" to the Drury Lane Theatre on March 19 and to Her Majesty's Theatre on March 22.)

Marian left the house on March 24. Chapman accompanied her to Euston Station and told her flatly, as he recorded in his diary, that he loved "E. [Elisabeth] and S. [Susanna], each in a different way." Marian burst into tears and abandoned the capital for the Midlands.

But Marian was too valuable to Chapman for him to break off relations. He persuaded her to write the prospectus for the new *Westminster Review*, which he planned to relaunch under his ownership as "an exponent of growing thought." The quarterly had been started by Jeremy Bentham and James Mill in 1824 as the voice of Philosophic Radicalism and liberal opinion, as a counterpoint to the conservative *Edinburgh Review*.

In 1837, Mill transferred the publication to his son, John Stuart Mill, who raised its reputation. High-minded and well written, it represented the avant-garde in skeptical science and literary reviewing, covering foreign as well as English books. Since it was transferred to a new owner in 1840, its budget had shrunk, its writers had deserted, and its circulation had dropped. Under his management, Chapman intended to feature the best writers and, without shocking public opinion, to cover "natural religion, natural morality and the laws of Nature." For the next few months, therefore, Marian and Chapman stayed in touch about his plans to acquire the magazine, and possibly about other matters. Knowing that Susanna would see her letters to him, Marian tucked inside the envelope small, personal, folded notes marked "to be thrown into the fire"—in other words, for his eyes only.[4]

In mid-1851, for £300, Chapman finally bought the *Westminster Review* and, with new backers, prepared to relaunch it at the end of the year, hoping to restore its former distinction. Marian was crucial to this plan. With the purchase nearly complete, Chapman went to Coventry and, according to his diary for May 1851, found "M. . . . shy, calm and affectionate." She was staying with the Brays, who, as usual, had fascinating guests—Mr. and Mrs. Thornton Hunt, who lived in a kind of commune in Bayswater that some dignified with the term phalanstery, which suggested that its women were, like agricultural land, property to be shared. Hunt was a well-known Radical, who, with the writer and philosopher George Henry Lewes, had founded the journal called *The Leader*. Their collaboration extended beyond their professional interests; Hunt fathered several children with

Lewes's wife, Agnes. She and Lewes already had had four of their own (one of whom died in infancy). Like the Brays, the liberated Hunts gave no thought to contraception. Hunt sired at least fourteen children.

Chapman's stay at Rosehill lasted thirteen days. He and Marian attended an amateur concert together, and it was noted that they left early. They wanted to talk about plans for the revamped *Westminster Review* and the conditions under which she could return to 142 Strand. He made it clear that his affair with Elisabeth Tilley was continuing; as he confessed to his diary, his passion went to "E."

While Chapman was in Warwickshire, Marian took him, as she had taken her friend D'Albert, to see the ruins of Kenilworth Castle near Coventry. The setting was so spectacular that Chapman started musing on the subject of beauty. "My words jarred upon her and put an end to her enjoyment," he recalled, with apparent regret. "Was it from a consciousness of her own want of beauty? She wept bitterly."

Before he had left for the Midlands, Chapman had negotiated a truce with his wife and mistress regarding Marian. Both accepted that she was essential to the success of his new venture. Elisabeth was the more resistant of the two; he assured her that she was fundamental to his happiness, and (if his record of sexual performance for the later months of 1851 can be trusted) he was true to his word. The détente allowed him to promise Marian an important job as editor if she would return to London. Her work would be compensated with free room and board at 142 Strand, and she would be paid extra for articles and reviews.

Marian accepted the deal. She apologized (or so he told his diary) for the pain she had caused on her earlier stay. Her new assignment was an attractive one—to write the long article on foreign literature in each issue. How could she resist? A challenging job as a writer in London was just what she hoped for.

*Chapter Five*

# WORKING JOURNALIST (1851–1852)

B Y THE END of September 1851, Marian was back at 142 Strand, in the same dark back room with its high, small window that gave just a glimpse of sky. She also had, as she requested, the same piano. Her return to the house was a tribute to her formidable ability, as well as to Chapman's power to convince his wife and his mistress that Marian was essential to the *Westminster Review*.

Marian had agreed to assume responsibility as editor of the review as long as her name was kept out of it. A female editor was as unheard of as a female surgeon; to be known to have one would have done no service to the review. Besides, her own inherent lack of confidence would have prevented her doing a good job if her name were to be attached.

So, anonymity once again. She suggested to Chapman how to manage the subterfuge: "With regard to the secret of the Editorship, it will perhaps be the best plan for you to state, that for the present you are to be regarded as the responsible person, but that you employ an Editor in whose literary and general ability you confide."

As an editor Marian was brilliant, with a quick eye for the redundant phrase, the weak argument, verbosity, the mixed metaphor. When Chapman himself submitted an article ("The Position of Woman in Barbarism and among the Ancients"), she was severe. " 'Stepping stones,' " she scolded, "cannot be 'forged into fetters.' " She reproved him for using "triads and duads of verbs and adjectives" and ducking into the subjunctive. Why did he use "would" instead of "is"?

She edited ten issues of the quarterly and succeeded in raising it to the stature it had held in the 1840s under John Stuart Mill. Hers was the perfect job for a woman in her ambiguous position: she could apply her intelligence to any subject and no one would know her name. Because of her wide reading, she could confidently commission articles on art, science, politics, religion, and foreign literature.

The audacious sweep of the *Westminster Review*'s subjects expressed the spirit of the time. No field was too specialized for the intelligent person's grasp. Everything was being rethought: religion, geology, slavery (and the American attitude toward it), women's rights, the status of Ireland, the place of classics in the school curriculum, the role of hereditary peers in the House of Lords. In addition, each issue of the quarterly carried about one hundred book reviews covering subjects ranging from contemporary literature to philosophy and science.

The *Westminster Review* was particularly adventurous on science. It tackled big issues that still resonate today: How does the brain work? What is memory? Were species designed or evolved? However, covering such controversial subjects came at a cost. It was branded as an "atheistic" publication and kept out of the lending libraries. Only 650 copies were printed of each issue, which sold for five shillings. But the *Westminster Review*'s reputation was strong, and it was even read in the United States.

All the articles, one must remember, were submitted in handwritten form. The typewriter was not invented until 1868 and even then was not widely used until later in the century. One of Marian's main tasks was deciphering often-illegible handwriting before she could even begin cutting articles down, shaping them into readable form, and occasionally informing the authors that the much-labored essay was not to be used after all.

Authors were anonymous, but they tended to know each other from the soirées Chapman held at 142 Strand almost every week. These were well attended not only by London literati but, in the early 1850s, also by European refugees from the political turmoil of 1848. Karl Marx is known to be among those who accepted Chapman's hospitality, but if he met Marian Evans, there is no record of it. Through Chapman she became friendly with some of the writers whose work she edited, including a regular contributor to the *Westminster Review*, Herbert Spencer.

The books and articles on philosophy, ethics, and science by Spencer and by George Henry Lewes show them to have been among the leading intellectuals in England at the time. By 1851, Lewes's publications included a four-volume *Biographical History of Philosophy*, published in 1845–1846. Spencer's first book was issued by Chapman in 1851 with the catchy title *Social Statics, or the Conditions Essential to Human Happiness Specified, and the First of Them Developed*. In it Spencer tried to delineate the rights of the individual as opposed to those of the state.

Lewes and Spencer shared a passion for science. Having met in 1850 through Chapman, the two men went out together to the botanical gardens at Kew to test Spencer's theories about plant species. On their walks, they discussed such topics as the division of labor by physiology and by social class. Chapman admired Lewes's versatility in swinging between art and science, writing two novels and a play as well as scientific and philosophical treatises. Lewes, for his part, was soon a convert to Spencer's theory of evolution.

"Survival of the fittest" was Spencer's own phrase, later acknowledged and adopted by Charles Darwin. His interest in its manifestation in human society was expressed (with a taste for alliteration tolerated by Marian, his editor) in one of the four articles on evolution he did for the *Westminster Review*. In April 1852 he wrote, "From the beginning, pressure of population has been the proximate cause of progress....It compelled men to abandon predatory habits and take to agriculture....It forced men into the social state."

In this article, called "A Theory of Population Deduced from the General Law of Animal Fertility," Spencer put forth the ideas that a universal factor in the development of species was the pressure of population and that those who continue the race are "those in whom the power of self-preservation is the greatest— the select of their generation." They were "select" because of their "inheritance of functionally-produced modifications"—a sign that Spencer, among others, was thinking along the same lines as Darwin in the 1850s. Spencer eventually persuaded Marian to create a new science section within the *Westminster*'s book reviews—indeed, to group all reviews by subject. However, the section called "Science" included the strange grouping of "Theology, History and Politics."

It was at William Jeff's bookshop in Burlington Arcade, Piccadilly, that in October 1851 Chapman first introduced Marian to George Henry Lewes. At first she was not impressed with the animated little man who talked all the time and waved his hands about. Writing to Charles Bray, who knew Lewes by reputation, she described him as "a sort of miniature Mirabeau"—a reference to the small Frenchman of fervid temperament who had been president of the Constituent Assembly in the French Revolution. But even then she knew Lewes not only as an historian of philosophy but also as a prolific journalist and critic. Not only had he had founded the lively weekly *The Leader* with his friend (and wife-sharer) Thornton Hunt, but he also contributed satirical pieces and theater reviews under the pseudonym Vivian.

Several months earlier, Marian had been introduced to Herbert Spencer when she visited London with the Brays to see the Great Exhibition in Hyde Park. He was a bachelor, a pleasant-looking fellow-Midlander, a year younger than she, and a journalist. He worked at *The Economist*, a new weekly (begun in 1843), with offices on the Strand, across from Chapman's house. Spencer shared her liberal sentiments—he was similarly opposed to slavery—and was a good conversationalist. He, like her, lodged above the shop; *The Economist*, as well as paying him a hundred guineas a year, gave him rooms at 340 Strand—a stretch of the Strand that led directly into Fleet Street before the creation of Aldwych and Kingsway at the start of the twentieth century. When he moved in, it took him a week "to become so far inured to the eternal rattle of the Strand as to be able to sleep."

Chapman's house at 142 Strand, near many publishers' houses, was a convenient base for American authors and book-buyers visiting London. *The Leader*, located nearby on Wellington Street, carried an advertisement describing "the Advantages of an Hotel with the Quiet and Economy of a Private Residence." However, the neighborhood was not entirely salubrious for a woman on her own. Marian was warned to keep away from the side streets leading off the Strand—narrow byways where drunks, beggars, prostitutes, and pornographic bookshops flourished (and still do).

Good as she was at her work, Marian was often depressed, preoccupied with her thoughts and worried about the lack of love in her life and her future. An American boarder at 142 Strand remembered her as appearing to live apart in her own world "of elevated thoughts and intense feeling." One morning he glimpsed her alone at the breakfast table, tears streaming down her face.

She left a happier memory with another lodger, William Hale White, a young editorial assistant on the *Westminster Review*, who had the room above her—a better one with a view over the south bank of the Thames. White (who later became the novelist Mark Rutherford) had abandoned clerical training for journalism after being expelled from Oxford for his Dissenting views of scripture and sin. He retained a picture of Marian Evans sitting in her dark room "with her hair over her shoulders, the easy chair half sideways to the fire, her feet over the arms, and a proof in her hands." "I never heard better talk than hers," White recalled. She was very kind to him—"a mere youth, a stranger, awkward and shy."

The *Westminster Review* issue of January 1852 was the first Marian edited. By the time of the second, she had begun to warm to London. As she wrote archly to Cara Bray, "I had two offers last night—not of marriage, but of music—which I find it impossible to resist. Mr. Herbert Spencer proposed to take me on Thursday to hear 'William Tell,' and Miss [Bessie] Parkes asked me to go with her to hear the 'Creation' on Friday."[1]

As a reviewer, Spencer enjoyed the journalistic perk of free tickets to theaters and concerts. And as a bachelor, he enjoyed having such a bright, perceptive, well-read companion at his side when he heard *Norma* and *I Martiri* and *Les Huguenots*. And Marian appreciated the privilege: "See what a fine thing it is," she wrote Cara self-mockingly, "to pick up people who are shortsighted enough to like one."

Working life was far from dull. In May 1852, there was an important meeting at 142 Strand. A distinguished group of authors including Wilkie Collins, Peter Roget, author of the new Thesaurus, and Spencer and Lewes, chaired by Charles Dickens, was protesting against the monopoly of the Booksellers Association, which claimed jurisdiction over the price even of imported American books. Chapman wanted to sell these at cost plus his own commission. Marian found Dickens's chairing excellent but his skull phrenologically disappointing—"the anterior lobe not by any means remarkable." Even so, the booksellers in attendance were humbled by the eminent authors and agreed to reconsider the harsh terms of their monopoly. At midnight she sat herself down at the piano and wittily thumped out "See, the Conquering Hero Comes" as a salute to Chapman's triumph.

Because of her work, Marian was often invited out. One host was Sir James Clark, physician to Queen Victoria. Another was Joseph Parkes, the Member of Parliament who had subsidized her *Das Leben Jesu* translation. His daughter Bessie, one of the first of many young women to have a crush on the older, formidably wise Marian Evans, left an appreciative description of her appearance as she descended the staircase of the family's mansion in Savile Row on her host's arm, wearing what was unusual for an unmarried woman—black velvet.

> She would talk and laugh softly, and look up into my father's face respectfully, while the light of the great hall-lamp shone on the waving masses of her hair, and the black velvet fell in folds about her feet... the upper part of the face had a great charm. The lower half was disproportionately long. Abundant brown hair framed a countenance which was certainly not in any sense unpleasing, noble in its general outline, and very sweet and kind in expression. Her height was good, her figure remarkably supple; at moments, it had an almost serpentine grace.

An even closer woman friend to Marian was Barbara Leigh Smith. Barbara's father was also a Radical Member of Parliament but, unlike Bessie's father, he was not married to her mother. Benjamin Leigh Smith fathered five children by the same woman but resisted marriage because of her low social status as a milliner. He himself, descended from a great Unitarian abolitionist, was a well-to-do patron of the arts and lived with his family in London at Blandford Square. Although he never legitimized his children, he did educate them and make them financially independent. Barbara used her money later to become one of the founders of Cambridge's first women's college, Girton. Once introduced, Marian took a great liking to Barbara, a gifted painter, and she was subsequently often asked to dine at the Leigh Smiths' lively dinners, at which she met Robert Noel, the brother of Edward, whom Cara Bray loved.

But what of Marian's feelings and personal life? Would anybody ever love her? She was moved by a passage from the newly published journal of Margaret Fuller, an American feminist who had just died after a late marriage. As an unmarried woman, Fuller had written, "I shall always reign through the intellect but the life! the life! O my God! shall that never be sweet?"

Yet, as 1852 wore on, Marian began to see more and more of Spencer. In May she wrote to Cara that "the brightest spot next to my love of old friends, is the deliciously calm new friendship that Herbert Spencer gives me. We see each other every day and have a delightful camaraderie in everything." Their jobs were remarkably similar, and she was an incomparable companion; she went with him not only to the theater but on a scientific expedition to Kew Gardens. Spencer liked her so much that he told his friend Edward Lott she was "the most admirable woman, mentally, I have ever met...the greatness of her intellect conjoined with her womanly qualities and manner, generally [keep] me at her side most of the evening." They walked together on the riverside terrace of Somerset House—she got a key from Chapman—and watched the boats on the Thames "on fine afternoons in May, June and July." At parties Chapman and Marian teased him about choosing him a wife.

In April 1852, Marian had written to Mr. and Mrs. Charles Bray of "my excellent friend Herbert Spencer," saying, "We have agreed that we are not in love with each other, and that there is no reason why we should not have as much of each other's society as we like. He is a good, delightful creature and I always feel better for being with him."

The Brays responded by inviting Spencer to Rosehill. Marian warned him that he should travel to Coventry by himself "for all the world is setting us down as engaged."

## Chapter Six

# FALLING IN LOVE AGAIN—AND AGAIN (1852–1854)

H ERBERT SPENCER FOLLOWED Marian's advice. Indeed, neither he nor Marian visited Rosehill that summer. In other respects, however, Spencer did little to quash rumors of an engagement between them. He visited her twice at Broadstairs on the Kent coast, where Marian had gone for a break after the July 1852 issue of the *Westminster Review* had gone to the printer. Her headaches were constant and she hoped the sea air would help, though it was unusual, she knew, for a woman to travel on her own. John and Susanna Chapman escorted her to the coast and saw her settled with rooms in a small cottage for a guinea a week, with a woman and a girl to look after her. In August, the Brays came to spend time with her. And, despite Marian's warning, so did Spencer, to judge from guarded comments in his autobiography.

Yet, much as he enjoyed her company, Spencer was embarrassed at the thought that he could be romantically associated with such an unattractive woman. In April he had written, "as delicately as I could," he told a friend, to make it clear that he was in no danger of falling in love with her and that he hoped that she would not fall in love with him.

It was too late; she already had. Her first response was a blithe letter, saying that it was "remote from [her] habitual state of mind" to imagine that anyone was falling in love with her. Yet her hopes persisted, as Spencer kept seeking her company. When he came down to Broadstairs in July, she handed him a letter shamelessly offering what amounted to a sexless marriage. Despite the subtle phrasing and psychological insight that foreshadow her great strengths as a novelist, the letter is painful to read:

> *I want to know if you can assure me that you will not forsake me, that you will always be with me as much as you can and share your thoughts and feelings with me. If you become attached to some one else, then I must die, but until then I could gather courage to work and make life valuable, if only I had you near me.... Those who have known me best have always said, that if ever I loved any one thoroughly my whole life must turn upon that feeling, and I find they said truly. You curse the destiny which has made the feeling concentrate itself on you—but if you will only have patience with me you shall not curse it long. You will find that I can be satisfied with very little, if I am delivered from the dread of losing it.*

She supposed, she said, that no woman had ever before written such a letter, but she was not ashamed, "for I am conscious that in the light of reason and true refinement I am worthy of your respect and tenderness, whatever gross men or vulgar-minded women might think of me."

The last remark shows that she knew already that others thought she was immoral. She said as much in another letter from Broadstairs to her young friend Bessie Parkes; if Bessie misbehaved, Marian would be blamed for it: "they lay it all to me and my bad influence over you." Such a reputation suggests that Bessie may have believed Marian had slept not only with Charles Bray, but also with John Chapman and possibly Dr. Robert Brabant.

The number of men in Marian's life did nothing to improve her sexual confidence. In her letters there are never more references to her ugliness, as her Yale biographer Gordon Haight points out, than during the time she was involved with Spencer. She described herself as "a hideous hag," "sad and wizened," and "haggard as an old witch." After six weeks on the coast, she returned to London resigned to the hopelessness of her love for Spencer, determined to move out of Chapman's house and make her way as a writer independent of him and independent of the *Westminster Review*.

⚜    ⚜

DURING the ensuing six months, however, there was a dramatic turn of events. Marian retreated from Spencer and transferred her affections to George Henry Lewes. Lewes appears to have taken the initiative. Spencer would sometimes bring Lewes with him when calling on Marian, and one afternoon, as Spencer rose to leave, Lewes stayed.

At first, Lewes had made an impression on Marian mainly because he talked too much. She wrote to the Brays that on her thirty-third birthday, when she had a racking headache and counted on having two clear hours until dinner to do some reading, there was a rap on the door: "Mr. Lewes—who of course sits talking till the second bell rings."

Lewes was a raconteur who followed one story with another, always complete with dialogue, accents, and hand gestures. (His grandfather had been a famous comic actor.) At Chapman's soirées there was always a circle around him.

His charm outshone his ugliness. Jane Carlyle, Thomas's wife, had nicknamed him Ape because of his narrow jaw, pock-marked skin, and wide cheekbones covered with facial hair. He was married with three sons, though by 1853 he and his wife Agnes were as good as separated. She already had two children by his business partner, Thornton Hunt, and was expecting another, and Lewes felt himself a free man. To save the new children from the stigma of illegitimate birth, or because it was the easiest course of action, he allowed them to be registered in his own name. In the eyes of the law, he thereby condoned his wife's adultery and so could never apply for a divorce. It was a decision that would have profound consequences not only for him, but also for Marian.

Following her rejection by Spencer, Lewes brightened Marian's life. He had as many free tickets as Spencer, and something better: entrée to the backstage world of the theater. As "Slingsby Lawrence," he was earning £10 per week writing or rewriting plays for the Lyceum Theatre, and wrote reviews, as "Vivian," for the weekly *Leader*. His journalistic output in itself was prodigious.

At the same time, Lewes was a serious author, prolific and erudite. Following his *Biographical History of Philosophy* in 1845–1846 and a biography of Robespierre in 1849, he had written a book on Auguste Comte, the French Positivist philosopher who wished to make the study of society a religion, and who coined the word "sociology." When Marian met Lewes, he was also writing a life of Goethe, a project for which his fluency in German served him well.[1]

Marian had discovered the love of her life. But their romance is difficult to document because she left behind no letters like her anguished plea for Spencer's love. One explanation is that from early 1853 until the end of Lewes's life in 1878, the two of them were virtually inseparable. Another is that, fearful of biographers, she directed that all Lewes's letters to her be buried with her when she died—an injunction that appears to have been obeyed.

&#8227;&#8239;&#8231;

FAMILY TROUBLES interrupted Marian's new relationship. In December 1852, she learned that her sister Chrissey's husband, Edward Clarke, had died, leaving her with six children and no money. Any inheritance Clarke had from his own father had been eaten up by debts, as had Chrissey's inheritance from her father's estate. The interest from the sale of his surgical practice, about £100 a year, was insufficient for their support.

Marian went back to the Midlands to try to help but soon fell to arguing with her brother over the best way to look after Chrissey and her children. Isaac had moved Chrissey and her family into the cottage in nearby Attleborough that Clarke had sold to Robert Evans when he needed money. After some weeks with her sister, Marian decided she could best help the stricken family by earning money and, without consulting her brother but with Chrissey's approval, decided to return to London to finish the proofs for the January 1853 issue of the *Westminster Review*. Isaac saw it as a selfish indulgence; he expected her to stay and help with Chrissey's children. Writing to the Brays and Sara Hennell, Marian described the argument:

> *Isaac, however, was very indignant to find that I had arranged to leave without consulting him and thereupon flew into a violent passion with me, winding up by saying that he desired I would never "apply to him for anything whatever"—which, seeing that I never have done so, was almost as superfluous as if I had said I would never receive a kindness from him.*

BACK IN LONDON, in January 1853, Marian announced to Chapman that she was moving out of 142 Strand and hoped soon to leave the *Westminster Review* itself. She told Charles Bray, rather ambiguously, that "many reasons, besides my health, concur to make me desire this change." Realizing how inconvenient it would be to lose her on-the-spot services, Chapman looked for a way to delay her move, offering her his own light, pleasant room in the communal house. She accepted and stayed until autumn.

If Chapman, as an experienced opener of bedroom doors, had previously wondered why he occasionally found Lewes in

Marian's room, he had no doubt about her feelings when, in December 1853, she lashed out at him for T. H. Huxley's hostile and sarcastic review of Lewes's book on Auguste Comte. In January of that year, she had also scolded Sara for failing to recognize that an article on atomic theory that appeared in the *Westminster Review* could not have been written by Lewes.

By the spring of 1853 Marian began to let her close friends know that Lewes had risen in her estimation. To Sara, she confessed that she now found Lewes genial and amusing: "He has quite won my liking, in spite of myself." In April, describing a visit to the theater with him, she told Cara Bray, "Mr. Lewes is kind and attentive and has quite won my regard after having a good deal of my vituperation." She had discovered that he was much better than he seemed, "a man of heart and conscience wearing a mask of flippancy." Indeed, the two were intellectual soul mates—each prodigiously well read in several languages.

New happiness did not relieve constant illness. Marian had suffered from headaches and depression since her schooldays, but now coughs, sore throats, and rheumatic pain in the shoulder kept her in bed for a week at a time. Her digestion was so bad, she said, she could hardly travel to Coventry "without a basin." Racked with pain, she tried the new anesthetic, chloroform, to have a tooth extracted. Despite her ailments, she loyally offered to accompany Chrissey and her family to Australia to see if they might find a new life there. Fortunately for her, Chrissey refused to budge.

In August, Marian went again to the Sussex coast, once more to St. Leonards. There is no explicit mention of Lewes in her holiday letters, but she did reveal that "Mr. Goethe is one of my companions here"—a coded reference to Lewes that must have amused her, even though her friends are unlikely to have picked it up. A new and defiant self-image began to emerge; in an earlier letter to Bessie Parkes, she wondered "whether it is sufficiently understood that I am a heathen and an outlaw."

On returning to London, Marian moved at last, on October 17, 1853, to 21 Cambridge Street, Bayswater, on the north side of Hyde Park. It was thanks to the money her father had left her that she could afford the move. Her new home, farther from the Thames and away from the thickest fog, consisted of two small rooms on the ground floor, for which she paid a hefty rent of £9 a month in contrast to her free room and board in the Strand. Her situation ensured that her visitors did not attract much notice, although she was startled by knocks on the front door, and she was unhappy about the sitting-room door, which didn't fit and let a draft in. Her landlady cooked her dinners. There was a piano she could use if she were not "too sick and headachy" to enjoy it.

Lewes visited her almost every day. Her letters to Sara are peppered with matter-of-fact asides such as "Mr. Lewes has just come in," or, apropos of some witty sayings, "Mr. Lewes dictated the greater number of them to me." Her health improved but his did not. Lewes had long suffered from distressing ailments such as a constant ringing in the ears, palpitations, and toothache, which frequent trips to supposedly health-giving places such as Malvern did not relieve. At times his health was so poor that his doctors ordered him not to write, and in April, Marian wrote to Cara that she had taken on some of Lewes's work on top of her own. From that time on, Lewes's pseudonyms were sometimes signed to reviews written by Marian Evans.

In early November, Marian declared to Charles Bray that "when I put my head into the house in the Strand, I feel that I have gained, or rather escaped a good deal physically by my change." At the end of the month she turned thirty-four and wrote to Sara, "I begin this new year more happily than I have done most years of my life."

Clearly, theirs was not a sexless love. Lewes was an experienced lover and Marian was ripe for awakening. Whoever had previously enjoyed her favors did so only fleetingly. Now she had a steady and confident man to guide her. What's more, if Lewes's wife and her fertile partner Thornton Hunt did not bother with contraception, Lewes the scientist did. Marian had told her worldly friend Barbara Leigh Smith, who'd had a brief affair with Chapman, that "in their intimate marital relationship he [Lewes] is unsensual, extremely considerate." It was plain to Barbara, as she wrote to Bessie Parkes, "that he makes her extremely happy."[2] It was clear also to Barbara that they practiced birth control and did not intend to have children.

Marian spent Christmas 1853 alone in Bayswater. She went to Chrissey's at the start of the New Year and then went on to Rosehill. With her she took her current project, a translation of *Das Wesen des Christentums* (*The Essence of Christianity*), by Ludwig Feuerbach. The book was another attack on orthodox Christianity and conventional morality, which allowed her to write about the philosophy of love and marriage that underlay her new life. She had accepted the translation as a commission from Chapman, and he had advertised the book as part of his new "Quarterly Series." She was finished with it by February, hoping she had eliminated the faults of heavy German prose, but was nonetheless convinced it would not sell. She knew that Chapman, deep in debt, would regret the £30 or so he was paying her for it, but she agreed completely with Feuerbach's ideas that "marriage as the free bond of love—is sacred in itself, by the very nature of the union which is therein effected." The sexual relation, thus defined, was the frankest expression of the divine in Nature.

At Cambridge Street over the months that followed, old friends visited: Bessie Parkes, Barbara Leigh Smith, even Spencer. He had quit *The Economist* after inheriting some money from an uncle and now, after some months on the Continent, returned to London to find the woman he had rejected firmly attached to his old friend Lewes.

Marian informed her half-sister, Fanny Houghton, in April 1854 that she was far from idle, being deep in proof-sheets and not "sitting with my hands crossed, ready to start for any quarter of the world at the shortest notice." Had she let slip a hint that she was about to go abroad with Lewes? Her health was better but she was very busy, having to do Lewes's work as well as her own. When he was ordered by his doctor to go to the country for ten days to relieve his ill health and was told not to write, she confided to Cara, "No opera and no fun for me for the next month!"

Almost as a deliberate insult to the happy couple, in April 1854 Herbert Spencer wrote for Lewes's own magazine, *The Leader*, a two-part essay titled "Personal Beauty." He praised beauty as a mark of evolutionary superiority and, correspondingly, related ugliness to mental and racial inferiority. As an example of ugliness, he gave an almost libelously graphic description of the face of Marian Evans. Abolitionist he may have been, yet he wrote that a projecting jaw "characteristic of negroes and, indeed, of all the lower human races, is a defect in a face," as were a wide mouth, a long mouth, and several other "peculiarities of feature which are by general consent called ugly." In an autobiography, published in 1904, Spencer continued the argument, by then conscious that he had spurned one of the most famous writers of the age: "Physical beauty is a sine qua non with me; as was once unhappily proved where the intellectual traits and the emotional traits were of the highest."

By the spring of 1854 Marian could not have cared less about Spencer's views of her physical attributes. She hinted to Charles Bray that her life was changing direction: "It is quite possible that I may wish to go to the Continent or twenty other things." In a long letter to his wife—Cara was still her close friend—she said, "My troubles are purely psychical-self-dissatisfaction, and [I] despair of achieving anything worth doing. . . . I can truly say they vanish into nothing before any fear for the happiness of those I love." She expected "to see Mr. Lewes back again to-day. His poor head—his only fortune—is not well yet."

Two months later, when Bray visited her in London on June 11, she confided in him her well-guarded secret—that she planned to go abroad with Lewes. Just over a month later, on July 14, she told him she was not leaving until the following Thursday. That he was clearly being kept closely informed and that Marian counted on him not to tell his wife seems to hint at past intimacy.

She lacked the courage to tell Cara and Sara directly of her audacious plan, knowing that the sisters did not like jokey little

Lewes; they disapproved of him partly because was married. Instead, she wrote tersely to Cara, Sara, and Charles on July 19: "Dear Friends,—all three—I have only time to say good-bye, and God bless you. Poste Restante, Weimar, for the next six weeks and afterwards Berlin." She offered no reason for the journey.

She was leaving England just before her Feuerbach book was to be published, with her name—Marian Evans—on the title page as translator. It would be the first and only time her real name was to appear on her work. *The Essence of Christianity* would present, in English, Feuerbach's humanistic argument that sexual relations are an expression of the divine. If marriage could be defined as a sexual union based on a mutual bond of love, Marian Evans and George Henry Lewes were married, and divinely happy.

*Chapter Seven*

# AN IDEAL HUSBAND (1854–1856)

"R AN OFF": London gossip would always use running images to describe the carefully planned departure of Marian Evans and George Henry Lewes for Germany on July 20, 1854. "I wonder what I had to run away from," Marian commented in her journal a month later after she had heard what people were saying. On the actual day of her departure, however, she must have had moments of doubt. She went alone to St. Katharine's Dock by the Tower of London and boarded the *Ravensbourne*, a steamer bound for Antwerp. It was a long twenty minutes before she saw Lewes's face over a porter's shoulder, and her new life began.

Crossing the Channel, the couple encountered Robert Noel, the freethinking brother of Cara Bray's beloved, Edward Noel. Marian knew him from dinners at Barbara Leigh Smith's and visits to Rosehill. Noel was en route to rejoin his wife, a German baroness, in Bohemia, after having visited the Brays in Rosehill. They found him a pleasant companion, although they may have wondered what he might write home about their elopement.

At Antwerp, with the high seriousness that would character-ize their life together, Marian and Lewes used every possible moment to look at art and architecture. She noted in her jour-nal that the *Elevation of the Cross* in the cathedral was "the fin-est conception of the suffering Christ I have ever seen," before departing the city for Liège on July 27.

On the railway platform at Liège, they ran into another familiar figure—Marian's old admirer, Dr. Robert Brabant. Attaching himself to them, he talked all the way to Cologne. Upon arrival at the city, however, he redeemed himself by introducing Marian to David Strauss, whose *Leben Jesu* she had translated. It was not a good meeting. In a discussion over breakfast at their hotel, Marian felt that Strauss was unhappy that she had used the fourth edition of his book for her trans-lation, one that he now saw as extreme and regretted; for her part, she wrote to Charles Bray, she found Strauss "strange and cast-down."

Cologne was Marian's first experience of the culture in whose language she had been immersed for ten years. She had the discomfort of realizing that, for all her knowledge, she could not speak German very well. En route to Weimar, they stopped in Frankfurt to see Goethe's house. They also looked over the *Judengasse*, the Jewish quarter, which Marian found "a striking scene." Despite her long interest in Judaism, going back to her purchase in 1838 of Josephus's *History of the Jews*, it was her first glimpse of the manner in which, in city after city, Europe's Jews had been confined.

Moving eastward, she found the Thuringian city of Weimar a disappointment. "How," she asked her journal, "could Goethe live here, in this dull, lifeless village?" But soon they discovered the park, the Schloss, and the glamorous inhabitants, notably the pianist and composer Franz Liszt, whom Lewes had befriended when he was living in Vienna in 1839. The couple admired the prominence given to the works of Richard Wagner in the repertoire of the Weimar opera house, the Court Theater. They agreed that they liked *Tannhäuser* and *The Flying Dutchman* but that *Lohengrin* was boring. Marian, with her long experience of housekeeping, was annoyed by the German beds with their eiderdowns "warranted not to tuck up."

Before long, Marian began to warm to the atmosphere of unpuritanical Europe, long a refuge for English fleeing the harsh moral climate at home. In Weimar, no one cared in the slightest whether or not she and Lewes had been through a marriage ceremony—least of all their friend Liszt. Director of the Court Theater and Kapellmeister to the Grand Duke of Weimar, Liszt was openly living with his vivacious mistress, Carolyne Sayn-Wittgenstein, the wife of a Russian prince. In her journal, Marian noted that the princess was short and stout, with blackish teeth. The two couples saw each other frequently and conversed in French.

Marian, although conscious of her gray hairs, was happier than she had ever been in her life. In Weimar she and Lewes had begun as they would go on, developing a working partnership of like-minded intellectuals: writing in the mornings, walking in the afternoons, reading aloud to each other in the evenings if not attending concerts or visiting friends. Everything that either of them wrote—or contemplated writing—was shared with the other. She told Bray (in another "Dear Friend" letter that hints at past intimacy) that she had had a month of "exquisite enjoyment" and seemed to have begun a new life. Bray was a "Dear Friend" indeed, having loaned her £50 against the next installment of her annual income, which her brother would pay in December.

Yet Marian also fully understood that her behavior was unconventional. As she wrote to John Chapman, she was prepared for the loss of all her friends. No matter. "I am not mistaken in the person to whom I have attached myself. He is worthy of the sacrifice I have incurred, and my only anxiety is that he should be rightly judged."

But Lewes, who had a reputation as a womanizer, would not be fairly judged; still less would she.

The news of Marian and Lewes's "elopement" was all over London and Edinburgh within a few weeks. Robert Tait, a Scottish writer and photographer who was in Weimar, learned from the headwaiter at his hotel that "a Mr. Lewes and his 'Sister'" had stayed at the hotel before they moved out to other lodgings but returned every day for the hotel's table d'hôte. Tait took it upon himself to visit the couple in their rooms and sent back to George Combe, the phrenologist, a full report detailing the arrangement of the adjoining bedrooms. Tait concluded that the circumstances were "suspicious," but he chose to think that Mr. Lewes would soon return to the wife and six children to whom he had said he was very attached.

As to Marian, might there be insanity in her family, Combe wondered, for "her conduct, with her brain, seems to me like morbid mental aberration"? There was no other way to account for "an educated woman who, in the face of the world, volunteers to live as a wife, with a man who already has a living wife and children" and who was pursuing a course "calculated only to degrade herself and her sex, if she be sane."

London was making good sport of the notorious "elopement" and, as befitted Victorian standards, it was the woman who got the blame. The word for such a woman was unprintable. Thomas Woolmer, a sculptor, wrote to one of Lewes's friends on October 4, 1854, that "blackguard Lewes has bolted with a —— and is living in Germany with her." The clergyman novelist Charles Kingsley less squeamishly referred to Marian as Lewes's "concubine." Marian's former dinner party host, the Radical Member of Parliament Joseph Parkes, after hearing the news of the elopement, came home, according to his daughter, "in a white rage, as if on the verge of a paralytic stroke" and forbade Bessie to have any further association with the immoral Marian Evans.

Not all their previous friends blamed Marian. On November 2, 1854, the philosopher Thomas Carlyle, who knew both runaways, wrote to his brother that Lewes had not only gone to Weimar, but was understood to have a "strong-minded woman" with him there: "He has certainly cast away his Wife here,— who indeed deserved it of him, having openly produced those dirty sooty skinned children which had Th[ornto]n Hunt as father[1] . . . Lewes to pay the whole account, even the money part of it!"

Carlyle wrote a sympathetic letter to Marian in Weimar to which Lewes replied, thanking him for not harshly misjudging her as so many were doing. He went on to explain his own case: "On my word of honour there is no foundation for the scandal as it runs. My separation was in no-wise caused by the lady named, nor by any other lady." He had been contemplating the change for some time, he said, "And I shall feel doubly bound to you if you will, on all occasions, clear the lady from such unworthy aspersions and not allow her to be placed in so totally false a position."

Marian herself made it clear to Chapman that she had not broken up the Leweses' marriage. Denying that Lewes "has run away from his wife and family," she declared that he had "never contemplated withdrawing the most watchful care over his wife and the utmost efforts for his children." And so it proved—even when she helped pay the bills.

But how was Marian to win back her Coventry women friends? Cara Bray and Sara Hennell had written her a letter saying they were hurt that she hadn't told them of her pending elopement. In return, she pleaded that she loved them all—Cara, Sara, and her sister, Chrissey—"the three women who are tied to my heart by a cord which can never be broken." Sara relented; Chrissey did not. Cara felt that proprieties should be respected. Marian's other ostensibly feminist friend, writer Harriet Martineau, despised Lewes and never spoke to Marian again.

If some friends were unable to forgive Marian's transgression, Chapman was no hypocrite. It would hardly have been possible for a womanizer like him to assume the moral high ground. Soon he would begin an affair with Marian's good friend Barbara Leigh Smith and would try to persuade her to live with him.[2] Rather than commenting on Marian's behavior, in his next letter, dated August 5, 1854, he asked her to write an article on the French philosopher Victor Cousin's *Madame de Sablé* for the next issue of the *Westminster Review*. She began it immediately.

However phlegmatic his correspondence with Marian, Chapman, knowing Lewes's fondness for women, wrote to a friend that he feared that Lewes might not stick with her: "I can only pray, against hope, that he may prove constant to her; otherwise she is utterly lost."

Marian and Lewes stayed in Weimar more than two months, their object to allow Lewes to research what became his excellent and well-received biography of Goethe. From Weimar, they shifted to Berlin in November. They stayed more than four months in the German capital, welcomed in the best artistic circles, going to the opera and museums, but fretting about their lack of freelance commissions. As her thirty-fifth birthday passed on November 22, 1854, Marian translated bits of Goethe for Lewes as well as continuing the translation she had begun in March 1849 during her father's last illness—Spinoza's 1677 book *Ethics*, which argued for the natural rights of man as a creature who is moved to perfect himself.

She also deepened her reading even further, especially in German and French. Her *Madame de Sablé* article for Chapman was a lively polemic on the superior lot of French women compared with that of their English sisters. "Woman in France: *Madame de Sablé*" appeared in October 1854 and praised the "delightful women of France," who, "from the beginning of the seventeenth to the close of the eighteenth century," wrote "what they saw, thought and felt." The result, Marian wrote (showing little foresight about what she herself would accomplish), was "that in France alone woman has had a vital influence on the development of literature." She was paid £15 for the article, a sum very helpful to the runaways' budget. She wrung another £20 from Chapman for an article on Carl Eduard Vehse's German-language *Memoirs of the Court of Austria*, a history of the Austrian monarchy and aristocracy, which appeared in the *Westminster Review* in April 1855.

Before sending off the French article, Marian had read it aloud to Lewes, who suggested that her ideas were crowded. The piece would read better, he said, if she thinned them out a bit. Acknowledging his critical judgment, she read him something else she had written: a description of a Staffordshire village and life in its neighboring farmhouses.

Why did she bring this fragment of manuscript along in the luggage she packed for Germany? There is no explanation beyond her observation in her journal that Lewes was struck with it as "a bit of concrete description." Perhaps, he suggested, she ought to try to write fiction.

In mid-March 1855 "the Leweses" endured three days in icy weather and a sickening, choppy Channel crossing on their return from eight months in Germany, to be welcomed by "English mutton, an English fire, and an English bed." They took lodgings at 1 Sydney Place, Dover. There Lewes left Marian and went up to London to sort out their next move.

Alone in Dover, walking on the cliffs, translating Spinoza, reading Shakespeare, reviewing books for Chapman, and writing an essay ("Three Months in Weimar") for *Fraser's Magazine*, Marian contemplated her future. If ever their love was to be tested, now was the time. What should Lewes do about his wife Agnes, who was pregnant again (by Thornton Hunt) and in debt? What kind of life could they make for themselves in London? Who would accept Marian now that she was a social outcast—and who would take her work? And where were they to live? Anxiety preyed on her, and while she waited for Lewes to return, Marian was never completely well. At the end of March she was confined to bed for two days with severe headaches and what she called "a bilious attack."

Besides Chapman, others also had doubts about Lewes's constancy. Marian's former friend Joseph Parkes told his daughter Bessie that Lewes was "a morally bad man" and feared he might "tire of & put away Miss Evans—as he has done others." Parkes had undoubtedly heard the rumor of Lewes's illegitimate child.

Chapman once more proved a true friend, offering Marian a regular assignment, reviewing contemporary literature for the Belles Lettres section of the *Westminster Review* for twelve guineas an issue and giving her the reassurance of a steady income.

For five weeks Marian waited alone on the Channel coast until Lewes sent for her to come to London. By mid-April he had done so. She had stipulated that Agnes must declare that she had no intention of returning to Lewes. Agnes responded emphatically, saying that there was no possibility of a reconciliation and she would be very happy if Lewes could marry Marian. Lewes had arranged lodgings at 8 Victoria Grove Terrace in Bayswater. (Presumably they exchanged letters during their separation, but none has survived.)

After only a brief time in Bayswater, however, the couple moved out along the railway line from Waterloo Station to 7 Clarence Row in the southwestern suburb of East Sheen, north of Richmond Park. As Marian explained to Bray in Coventry,

> *we go tomorrow to our new home at East Sheen, a charming village close to Richmond Park...it will be a pleasure to you to see that pretty place and it is far less trouble to get there than to Bayswater. You have only to jump into the train at the Waterloo Bridge Station and in ten minutes you will be at Mortlake where you must get down. Mortlake, as I daresay you know, is a lovely village on the banks of the Thames, and East Sheen is its twin sister lying close to it. Ask the way to East Sheen and in three minutes you will be at our door. Then you shall have a nice dinner and a nice snooze after it, and then a stroll, along the river or in the Park, such as you can't get at Coventry even by the help of a carriage.*

Happy with the proximity of the railway and the park, Marian stayed clear of London while Lewes, untainted by scandal in a man's world, enjoyed himself at dinners and parties as before. She wrote a number of articles that Lewes placed for her as "the work of a friend."

Both worked hard to earn money: Agnes, with her growing brood, had run up heavy debts for which Lewes was legally liable. He gave her an annual sum of £250 for support. In the first summer after his return from Germany he took his three sons, now ages nine, eleven, and thirteen, to Ramsgate for a week. He never forsook them.

Like Marian, Lewes was never completely well. He was plagued with chronic illnesses similar to hers—headache, neuralgia, indigestion. Marian, as a working journalist, described his condition in July 1855 to Sara Hennell: "Mr. Lewes is still sadly ailing—tormented with tooth- and face-ache. This is a terrible trial to us poor scribblers, to whom health is money, as well as all other things worth having. I have just been reading that Milton suffered from indigestion—quite an affecting fact to me."

In sickness or in health, Marian poured out brilliant articles. Among these was a brief review of *An Account of the Life, Opinions and Writings of John Milton*, by Thomas Keightley, which appeared in *The Leader* on August 4, 1855. As the article was anonymous, she could use it to vent her anger at the near-impossibility of divorce, a subject also close to Milton's heart. In his 1643 essay *Doctrine and Discipline of Divorce*, she explained, Milton argued

> that a true marriage was of mind as well as of body.... Milton's plea for divorce, of course, drew down on him plenty of Presbyterian vituperation: his book was "a wicked book," his error "too gross for refutation." Yet his style is singularly calm and dignified. He desires...that some conscionable and tender pity might be had of those who have unwarily, in a thing they never practised before, made themselves the bondmen of a luckless and helpless matrimony.

Marian spelled out her own philosophy on divorce to Cara Bray, in a letter trying to appease the old friend who now rejected her. If there was one subject, she wrote emphatically, "on which I feel no levity it is that of marriage and the relation of the sexes." The last thing she wanted was "light and easily broken ties.... Women who are satisfied with such ties do not act as I have done—they obtain what they desire and are still invited to dinner."

Despite her attempts to win back friends, Marian was becoming more vehement in her contempt for conventional religion. In August 1855 she surpassed herself by composing a scathing attack in the *Westminster Review* on a popular Scottish evangelist, Dr. John Cumming, who was drawing throngs to his church in Covent Garden. Her unsigned article portrayed the preacher as vain, lazy, ill-read, illogical, and posturing. The powerfully worded article, which appeared in October 1855 and ran more than thirty pages, was widely noticed. "Evangelical Teaching: Dr. Cumming" was the liveliest of the writer's assaults on the religion of her adolescence. Bray guessed that she was the author.

She was not pleased at being found out and begged Bray to keep her secret. The article appears to have made a strong impression, one which would be a little counteracted if the author were known to be a woman—and a fallen woman at that.

The essay made a strong impression on Lewes as well. One day as they walked in Richmond Park, he told her he was now convinced of her true genius as a writer. He pressed his earlier suggestion, now with some force: "You must try and write a story." If her fiction were as good as her journalism, he reasoned, she could make money from it. He would help her; as a playwright, he knew about drama and dialogue. He was in no way envious of her ability. His two-volume *The Life and Works of Goethe* was about to come out with the London publisher David Nutt, to acclaim and good sales, and he was turning his attention to evolutionary science—to marine biology in particular.

Before Marian took up his suggestion, they moved slightly to the west to Richmond, and in October 1855 took rooms at 8 Park Shot, a Georgian terrace between the Green and the railway station, not far from the famed view of the winding Thames from Richmond Hill.

Marian needed a new direction, because it seemed unlikely that her nearly completed translation of Spinoza's *Ethics* would be published. Lewes's informal agreement with a London publisher, H. G. Bohn, fell apart. Bohn, who had brought out Lewes's book on Comte, backtracked on his original offer to bring out the Spinoza and after acrimonious correspondence, Lewes withdrew in anger. Marian was left with nothing (in money or print) to show for fifteen months' hard work on a huge and difficult manuscript.

And so, in September 1856, Marian dipped into her Midlands and evangelical past, with its bitter religious factions, and began writing a short story based on a clergyman she had known at Chilvers Coton church. Renaming him Amos Barton, she set him in a fictionalized Warwickshire called Loamshire. Titled "The Sad Fortunes of the Reverend Amos Barton," the story told of a hard-pressed, unpopular clergyman who earns his parishioners' affections after the death of his beautiful, gentle, overworked, child-burdened wife, Milly. Lewes sent it off to John Blackwood in Edinburgh, fearing Marian's handwriting might be recognized by London editors. He told Blackwood the author was "a friend." It was the beginning of a working arrangement between Lewes and Marian that was to last the rest of their lives, in which George Lewes served as Marian's inspiration, her critic, her counselor, and, not least, her literary agent.

This was never as true as in his management of her first work of fiction. Blackwood had published some of Lewes's own stories and was preparing to bring out *Sea-side Studies*, a long scientific series based on Lewes's new passion for collecting and classifying mollusks and sea anemones. A pleasant-looking Scot in his thirties, Blackwood was the sixth son of the founder of the Blackwood imprint. He was, in fact, religious and conservative enough to have been deterred by Marian's irregular status—had he known of it.

Lewes sent "Amos Barton" off to Edinburgh the day after Marian finished it. In his covering letter, he said that at the outset he had harbored "considerable doubts of my friend's power as a writer of fiction," but these doubts were transformed into high admiration upon reading the manuscript.

Blackwood felt the same. Despite a few reservations, he concluded his reply by saying, "I am happy to say that your friend's reminiscences of Clerical Life will do." He also asked to see more—the request that launched George Eliot.

*Chapter Eight*

# HOUSE OF TWO GEORGES (1857–1859)

"THE SAD FORTUNES of the Reverend Amos Barton" appeared in January and February 1857 in *Blackwood's Edinburgh Magazine*, the influential monthly that John Blackwood and many readers fondly called *Maga*. This first story alone brought Marian, for a month's writing, the welcome sum of fifty guineas (about $5,300 in today's money). It was a considerable sum for the Leweses who, as a couple, had been strained by Agnes's debts and were living at the time in one room, sometimes with only bread and butter for lunch.

Blackwood wanted to know the name of the author, but Lewes wouldn't say. Frustrated, on January 30, 1857, Blackwood addressed a letter to "My dear Amos," enclosing the concluding part of the published "Amos Barton." Marian had been upset by some of John Blackwood's comments about the "sniffing and dirty noses" in her story, quibbles that implied it contained perhaps rather too much realism. (It was a hypersensitivity to criticism that would last all her life.)

A response to his letter was required, however, so she replied, artfully concealing her gender, in a letter to Blackwood's brother and colleague, Major William Blackwood, thanking him for his generosity. "I am very sensitive to the merits of cheques for fifty guineas," she wrote, "but I am still more sensitive to that cordial appreciation which is a guarantee to me that my work was worth doing for its own sake." She signed herself "The Author of Amos Barton." About a month later, she insisted to him once more, "Whatever may be the success of my stories, I shall be resolute in preserving my incognito.... Perhaps, therefore, it will be well to give you my prospective name, as a tub to throw to the whale in case of curious inquiries, and accordingly I subscribe myself, best and most sympathizing of editors, Yours very truly, George Eliot."

This was the first appearance of the name which subsequently appeared on all her work. She chose it as a nom de plume, she later said, because George was Mr. Lewes's Christian name, and Eliot was "a good mouth-filling, easily-pronounced word." It so happened that she also had a grandfather and an uncle named George, and there had been a George Eliot Close on a seventeenth-century map of Chilvers Coton in her father's office at Griff House. The name, what is more, echoed the male disguise of the scandalous French novelist George Sand, who portrayed the struggles of women against a repressive society.

It was common at the time, although not obligatory, for women writers to use pseudonyms. Jane Austen's first novel,

*Sense and Sensibility*, appeared in 1811 as the work of "A Lady," Charlotte Brontë's *Jane Eyre* in 1847 as the work of Currer Bell. Lewes, who had favorably reviewed the latter novel for *Fraser's Magazine*, was suspicious of the name and suggested that it cloaked the fact that the author was a woman. Elizabeth Gaskell and Harriet Martineau, however, both wrote under their own names and had great success.

*Scenes of Clerical Life* appeared in book form in January 1858, in two volumes, with a print run of one thousand. Mudie's, the largest of the lending libraries from which many people borrowed books to avoid the high cost of purchase, took 350 copies. Nearing forty, Marian Evans was now an author.

Constructing her tales with Midlands scenes and with some characters using broad Warwickshire dialect, Marian was following the doctrine of realism according to John Ruskin's *Modern Painters*: "the doctrine that truth and beauty are to be attained by a humble and faithful study of nature," as she summarized it in *Westminster Review*. But Marian's gift went beyond describing physical details and reproducing local voices. She conveyed the inner feelings and thoughts of her characters in a way that brought them alive to the reader.

The three clerical stories of the book *Scenes of Clerical Life* are full of feeling—not the kind of dry, polysyllabic prose Marian had been pouring into the *Westminster Review*. The three are all sad stories, death providing resolution to each plot. The title of the first, "The Sad Fortunes of the Reverend Amos Barton," was ironic for an account of the misfortunes of the clergyman who saw his gentle wife Milly die from overwork and the strain of bearing seven children.

Lewes, reading the deathbed scene in which the broken-hearted vicar sobs over the body of his wife, was moved to tears. He told Marian, "your pathos is better than your fun." He was not alone in his reaction. An author whom John Blackwood admired, Albert Smith, wrote to him, saying, "The death of that sweet Milly made me blubber like a boy. I did not think, at forty, I had so many tears left in me."

"Mr. Gilfil's Love Story," second in the sequence, concerns another parson, this one modeled on the Reverend Bernard Gilpin Ebdell, who was vicar of Chilvers Coton church until 1828 and had baptized Marian in 1819. The fictional Mr. Gilfil, chaplain to the local great house Cheverel Manor (clearly drawn from the Arbury Hall that dominated Marian's youth), is in love with a girl who loves another; he convinces her to marry him only after her beloved dies, but she herself dies soon after.

The third story, "Janet's Repentance," tells of an evangelical clergyman, the Reverend Edgar Tryan, whose parishioners include Janet, a woman driven to drink by her brutal husband. The parson guides Janet away from alcohol, and after her husband dies she devotes her life to the service of others. The first part of "Janet's Repentance" was published in *Blackwood's* on July 1, 1857. This last story alone brought Marian £121 (about $12,000 today).

In all, Marian received £433 9 shillings 2 pence for the book and its serialization. Blackwood made the checks out to Lewes. Early on, Lewes had informed Blackwood that the new author suffered from a hypersensitivity to criticism and lack of self-confidence, problems that would become chronic: it took all Lewes's efforts to encourage his friend and to protect him from any shadow of disapproval.

By May 1857, Marian had been confident and prosperous enough to inform Isaac, Chrissey, and her half-sister, Fanny, that—at least insofar as she was concerned—she was married. She also asserted her status as Mrs. Lewes, a title she felt she deserved more than Agnes Lewes, who had just given birth to her fourth child by Thornton Hunt.

From the island of Jersey, where she accompanied Lewes "zoophyte hunting" in search of marine specimens, Marian wrote:

*My dear Brother*

*You will be surprised, I dare say, but I hope not sorry, to learn that I have changed my name, and have someone to take care of me in the world. The event is not at all a sudden one, though it may appear sudden in its announcement to you. My husband has been known to me for several years, and I am well acquainted with his mind and character. He is occupied entirely with scientific and learned pursuits, is several years older than myself, and has three boys, two of whom are at school in Switzerland, and one in England.*

She told Isaac they would probably be spending the winter in Germany and asked if he would be kind enough to pay her income from the money left in trust by her father to the account of Mr. G. H. Lewes, into the Union Bank of London, Charing Cross Branch, 4 Pall Mall East. They were not rich people, she added, but were both workers and had enough for their needs. She signed herself "Your affectionate Sister Marian Lewes."

Isaac Evans responded only with a solicitor's letter demanding to know when and where the marriage had taken place. She replied to the solicitor, Vincent Holbeche, with essential legal information: Mr. Lewes was a well-known writer of, among other things, *Life and Works of Goethe*; she had been his wife and borne his name for nearly three years; their marriage was not a legal one but regarded by them both as a sacred bond. Any money due her was to be paid into his Union Bank account. In conclusion, she thanked Holbeche for having suggested to her father when drawing up his will that he leave her £100 in cash rather than household goods, specifically to provide for her in the year after his death.

In the weeks that followed, Chrissey's little daughter Fanny died, and Marian's high spirits deflated. By the time the Leweses returned from Jersey, she was in a curious state of poor health and grief. Still, she managed on July 2, 1857, to be a bridesmaid at a London wedding—once again at a Unitarian Chapel—for her friend Barbara Leigh Smith, who, having thrown over John Chapman, was marrying Dr. Eugene Bodichon, a Breton who lived in Algiers. Thus, for one of Marian's best women friends, the stigma of illegitimacy (and of having a milliner for a mother) was overcome.

In December 1857, William Blackwood visited Richmond and believed he would have the chance to meet George Eliot there. But it was not to be; Lewes made the excuse that the author was too timid. However, William wrote to his brother John that he did meet "a Mrs. Lewes." Marian worried that he might suspect that she was George Eliot, but William did not guess the truth. Lewes did the talking, focusing on his own experience with the Blackwoods and saying they were the most agreeable publishers he had ever dealt with. He was pleased that the firm had accepted his own new book, *Physiology of Common*

*Life*; the first part was about to be published in *Blackwood's*. He strove to keep up the fiction of George Eliot's maleness. Having heard John Blackwood's account that the rector of a large parish had cried like a child over "Janet's Repentance," Lewes declared, "If a few more rectors would be equally tearful I think E. [Eliot] would at last really begin to believe in his power."

On Christmas Day, 1857, the couple ate turkey and walked in Richmond Park, where the air was so clear they could see across London to Hampstead. Their happiness was compounded by the fact that Marian's first book looked set to be a success. When Lewes read from it at the home of one of his best friends (the writer Arthur Helps, with whom he was staying the week after Christmas), Marian wrote happily in her journal that "they were all sure I was a clergyman." On New Year's Eve, 1857, she wrote,

> *My life has deepened unspeakably during the last year. . . . And my happiness has deepened too: the blessedness of a perfect love and union grows daily. . . . Few women, I fear have had such reasons as I have to think the long sad years of youth were worth living for the sake of middle age. . . . So goodbye, dear 1857! May I be able to look back on 1858 with an equal satisfaction of advancement in work and heart.*

More satisfaction was to follow. Lewes came home on January 2, 1858, with a highly favorable *Times* review in his pocket; the editor had requested an early copy of the book. On January 5, soon after *Scenes of Clerical Life* came out, the most famous author of the day, Charles Dickens, wrote a fan letter to "George

Eliot." He had read the first two tales in the *Scenes of Clerical Life*, which he had received through the Blackwoods, and wished to express his "admiration of their extraordinary merit. The exquisite truth and delicacy, both of the humour and the pathos of those stories, I have never seen the like of." He was almost tempted to address the author as a woman, he joked, because "no man ever before had the art of making himself mentally so like a woman since the world began."

While Dickens may have suspected the truth, many readers of *Scenes of Clerical Life* assumed the author to be a clergyman. Some detected a woman's touches, however, while local readers quickly picked up allusions to family places and translated the fictional town of Milby to Nuneaton. A list was even circulated naming the alleged originals of various characters. Charles Newdigate Newdegate, now Conservative Member of Parliament for North Warwickshire, accosted the publisher John Blackwood at Epsom on Derby Day, May 29, 1858, and congratulated him for publishing a "capital series...all about my place and County."

By this time, John Blackwood had been brought in on the secret of his author's identity, a full year after he had given George Eliot to the world. On a visit to London, on February 28, 1858, Blackwood went out to Richmond and again asked, in Marian's presence, if he might at last meet George Eliot. Ever the showman, Lewes made a parlor game of the encounter, asking, "Do you wish to see him?"

"As he likes," said Blackwood. "I wish it to be quite spontaneous." Marian left the room, followed by Lewes, and agreed to go through with the revelation. The pair came back and Blackwood was introduced to "George Eliot." What he saw, he wrote to his wife, was "a most intelligent pleasant woman, with a face like a man, but a good expression."

Blackwood returned to Richmond a week later and told the Leweses that his wife (as well as the novelist William Thackeray) was still convinced that *Scenes of Clerical Life* could not have been written by a woman. By then Marian, writing as George Eliot, was well into a new book, based on the terrible story she had heard twenty years earlier from her aunt, the Methodist preacher Elizabeth Evans, about a girl condemned for killing her newborn child. It was to be a serial novel, and by the end of January 1858 she had already completed eight chapters. She told Blackwood on January 9, 1858, that she had read the early chapters to Lewes, and he had said it was her best work so far. The couple walked with him to nearby Kew and after Marian had given Blackwood some of her new novel, *Adam Bede*, they parted on friendly terms. Blackwood read the chapters on the train back to Edinburgh and pronounced them "most lifelike and real."

Despite Marian's success with *Scenes of Clerical Life*, money remained a concern. Agnes's debts were rising, to Lewes's distress, so for reasons of economy as well as research, the Leweses went to Germany from April 11 until July 7. Marian wrote nearly two-thirds of *Adam Bede* in Munich and Dresden before returning to London in September to finish it in their rooms at Park Shot, Richmond.

They had chosen a good summer to be out of London: 1858 was the year of the Great Stink, when the Thames, then essentially an open sewer, clouded the city with noxious fumes. While they were away, on May 29, 1858, an excellent review of Marian's stories appeared in the *Saturday Review* praising *Scenes of Clerical Life* for its boldness, originality, humor, and pathos, deducing that the pseudonym cloaked "some studious clergyman, a Cantab, who lives, or has lived the greater part of his life in the country, who is the father of a family, of High Church tendencies, exceedingly fond of children, Greek dramatists, and dogs."

Despite their need for economy, as she later wrote to Blackwood, "I don't want the world to give me anything for my books except money enough to save me from the temptation to write only for money." That was true, but only in part. Her fiction gave her imagination a chance to live again in Warwickshire, to dip back into what she later called "the memory of that warm little nest where my affections were fledged."

In *Adam Bede*, set in 1799, she rescued more than the nest. The novel featured her father's occupation, the titled gentry, the great house, the canal, the mines, the clergy, the social and religious divisions, the dialect, the dogs, the smell of wood shavings, and, as if bringing him back to life, her father himself: the tall, stalwart workman with dark eyes indicating a touch of Celtic blood and an iron grasp that could shake the soul out of an unruly laborer. Her estranged brother, Isaac, when he had read the book, told Sara Hennell that nobody but his sister could have written it—especially the passages about their father.

Like one of the Dutch or Flemish painters she had so admired in Belgian and German museums, Marian believed in getting every humble domestic detail right so the picture could speak for itself. She caught the rhythm of the agricultural year, the rural parties, the country dancing, the sounds and cadences of local speech, the kinds of wildflowers and cheeses, and the furnishings of a farmhouse, as in this passage from *Adam Bede*:

> Hetty Sorrel often took the opportunity, when her aunt's back was turned, of looking at the pleasing reflection of herself in those polished surfaces, for the oak table was usually turned up like a screen, and was far more for ornament than for use; and she could see herself sometimes in the great round pewter dishes that were ranged on the shelves above the long deal dinner-table, or in the hobs of the grate, which always shone like jasper.

It was an astonishing achievement for someone who, hardly two years before, had not thought of herself as a novelist.

Set in the fictional village of Hayslope, the plot of *Adam Bede* centered on the seduction of the vain and pretty Hetty Sorrel, niece of the genial farmer Martin Poyser. Hetty is loved by Adam Bede, the respected village carpenter, but is seduced by the young squire Arthur Donnithorne. When rejected by him, she agrees to marry Adam but then finds that she is pregnant. As her time draws near, she flees to find Arthur, but gives birth in a wood. She covers the baby with grass and chippings but thinks she hears it cry all night; going back in the morning, she finds it dead. Arrested for infanticide and condemned to death, she is visited in her cell by Dinah Morris, who is modeled on Marian's aunt Elizabeth Evans. Unlike the real case, where the condemned girl died on the gallows, Hetty is reprieved and sentenced to transportation (a seemingly humane solution in the days before it was recognized how females suffered on the ships carrying them to the Antipodes).

As Marian's work on the novel progressed, Lewes showed once again what an invaluable mate he was. He knew that plot was not her strong point. Her gift was psychological characterization and the interrelatedness of actions: she displayed an almost scientific sense of determinism in showing how one person's actions affected another. But to move the story along, Lewes suggested that Adam and Arthur, the carpenter and the aristocrat, should fight each other over Hetty. Lewes also suggested the final dramatic resolution of the plot—to have the preacher Dinah marry Adam Bede and give up her preaching. This plot resolution by self-effacement, following that in "Janet's Repentance," placed Marian firmly on the course of ratifying woman's renunciation of ambition; something that would later dismay feminist readers. Yet, using the kind of careful research she enjoyed, Marian found a sound historical reason for having Dinah abandon her ministry for wifehood: in 1803 the Methodists, who early in their movement had encouraged female preachers, stopped women from addressing any but their own sex.

Lewes also, of course, offered constant encouragement during Marian's periods of depression and worked hard to prevent her from seeing any criticism or bad reviews. Not that there were any bad reviews. Blackwood had been concerned by the sexual sin at the heart of the plot, but he needn't have worried. Published at the beginning of February 1859, *Adam Bede* was an instant success. The *Times* declared that its author "takes rank at once among masters of the art," continuing to note that no one knew the real name of the author and that it was even being suggested that the author must be a lady. Within four months Queen Victoria had read it, having enjoyed *Scenes of Clerical*

*Life* a year earlier. She commissioned paintings of Hetty churn-
ing butter and Dinah preaching, and recommended the novel
to her uncle, King Leopold I of Belgium, and her daughter,
Princess Louise. Twenty-one hundred copies were printed of the
first edition, which sold for 31 shilling 6 pence each. Mudie's
took a thousand. Reprinted in a 12-shilling form, the book sold
ten thousand copies in its year of publication. French, German,
Dutch, Russian, and Hungarian editions followed. It outsold
*A Tale of Two Cities.*

Marian's success was darkened six weeks later by the news
that Chrissey had died from consumption. She had planned to
visit her sister during her illness and hoped to heal their long
estrangement, but Chrissey had sent her a penciled note saying
that she feared she could not stand the strain of a reunion. The
death, Marian wrote to Sara, "has taken the possibility of many
things towards which I looked with some hope and yearning. I
had a very special feeling towards her, stronger than any third
person would think likely."

*Adam Bede* effectively bought the Leweses a house. In
November 1858, Blackwood offered £800 (about $90,000
today) for copyright of the book for four years. Four days after
publication, on February 11, 1859, the Leweses took a seven-year
lease on half of a four-story villa on Wimbledon Park Road in
Wandsworth. The house, Holly Lodge, needed furniture, cur-
tains, and beds, and the couple intended that Lewes's boys, when
not at school, would stay with them, relieving Agnes's crowded
household. The two older boys were in Switzerland at Hofwyl, a
progressive school near Berne, where the Noel brothers had been
educated. For Lewes, Holly Lodge was a proper home at last, one

into which he could move his books and possessions from the house he had shared with Agnes. Marian was relieved to have private space at last. In Richmond, she and Lewes had worked at separate tables in the same room; she found the scratching of his pen "nearly drove her wild." Her writing benefited almost immediately from the change of circumstances. By the end of April she had completed a short story with a mystical twist, "The Lifted Veil," begun, she said, on a morning "when my head was too stupid for more important work."

Holly Lodge, halfway between Putney and Wandsworth railway stations, brought another suburban advantage: neighbors. Nearby lived the Congreves, Richard and his much younger wife, Maria, who called on them because they too had Coventry connections: Maria's father was a doctor who had looked after Robert Evans.

Maria became another in the long line of young women who would as good as fall in love with Marian, a line that grew with the fame of George Eliot and the appreciation of her books.

Richard Congreve was an ex-clergyman who embraced Positivism—a secular religion founded by Auguste Comte, the subject of Lewes's book, *Comte's Philosophy of the Sciences.* Positivism encouraged the worship of humanity and observable fact and sought the scientific perfectibility of life on earth. It abandoned the search for the soul or for an "ultimate purpose" for mankind. According to Positivist thought, eternal life was real only in that the dead remain alive in the memories of the living.

Marian's circumstances had improved considerably, but she still hoped to avoid public recognition as the author of the novels that had made her fortune. Public debate continued as to who had written *Adam Bede*, and Marian's disguise was shaken by the insistence of many Midlands people that they had found identifiable people in her fiction. She was insulted by the implication that she did no more than copy from life. However, as long as she sought to remain anonymous, she could do little to defend herself—either against criticism, or against false claims to her pseudonym. One Midlander was increasingly insistent that he was the author of *Adam Bede*. His name was Joseph Liggins.

Liggins's claim reached the press when a letter appeared in the *Times* on April 15, 1859, written by a Reverend Henry Anders, declaring that the true name of the author of *Adam Bede* was Joseph Liggins, of Nuneaton, Warwickshire, and that Blackwood had cheated Liggins out of his rightful earnings for his work. Soon a fake manuscript of the book in Liggins's hand began to circulate and a local fund was started to compensate Liggins for deprivation of his rightful earnings. Liggins, who lived in Attleborough near Nuneaton, was real enough: a baker's son who had been sent down from Cambridge. He had claimed earlier that he had written *Scenes of Clerical Life*. Marian and Lewes had laughed it off, but Liggins had persisted in his claim and now renewed it with *Adam Bede*.

To support his partner, Lewes himself sent a letter from "George Eliot" to the *Times* on June 25, calling Liggins an imposter and swindler and declaring that "he," the real author, was being denied the courtesies extended to gentlemen simply because he chose to withhold his name.

The scandal grew to the point that both Blackwood brothers paid a visit to Holly Lodge. They agreed to abandon George

Eliot's incognito. Tensions now centered on the deal for the new novel, which became *The Mill on the Floss*.

But the truth was not widely known. On November 5, Herbert Spencer came out to Wandsworth with a question from John Chapman: Had Marian written *Adam Bede*? Spencer had responded with silence when Chapman asked him. He had already guessed the answer; three years before, on a visit to Richmond, when he had suggested that Marian ought to try writing fiction, she had let slip that she had already begun "Amos Barton." On visiting the couple this time, however, Spencer was annoyed that they expected him to lie outright.

Realism may have been Marian's artistic credo, but both Leweses were unrealistic to the point of irrationality in trying to hide the truth. Lewes appears to have forgotten that he had tried to blow Charlotte Brontë's cover in his review of *Jane Eyre* for *Fraser's Magazine*. The dispute soured their friendship with Spencer for many months.

The break with Chapman that followed was irreparable. Both Leweses felt that he had been indelicate in not respecting their wish for anonymity. Lewes wrote to Chapman with a flat denial: "she authorizes me to state, as distinctly as language can do so, that she is not the author of *Adam Bede*." Marian wrote in her journal that she wanted nothing more to do with him. She took revenge by refusing her consent for Chapman to republish her articles from the *Westminster Review*.

Marian may have been determined to hide her authorship, but all who knew the Leweses noticed the rise in their standard of living. The exchange of small rented rooms for a large house with furniture, linens, and servants could only mean a new source of income.

Barbara Bodichon (formerly Leigh Smith), living in Algiers with her doctor husband, guessed the secret herself simply from reading newspaper reviews of *Adam Bede* and wrote to Marian that she had instantly recognized her voice, views, and sensibilities. To Marian this was the first instance of "detection on purely internal evidence" and she asked Barbara to promise to keep her secret safe. A month later she assured William Blackwood that only one person knew for a fact who George Eliot was.

By the end of June, Marian had at last made peace with the Brays and Sara Hennell over her relationship with Lewes and told them the truth. But she begged them not to say that they knew the author or to discuss her work with her: "Talking about my books has the same malign effect on me as talking of my feelings or my religion."

To Charles Bray, in another letter, she confided that all she wanted her books to achieve was that "those who read them should be better able to imagine and feel the pains and joys of those who differ from themselves in everything but the broad fact of being struggling erring human creatures." She signed herself "G.E." but in a postscript declared, "My name is Marian Evans Lewes."

This self-imposed confusion over Marian's name clouded both her personal and professional lives. Lewes flew into a rage when Barbara Bodichon addressed an envelope to Marian Evans. He reminded Barbara: "that individual is extinct, rolled up, mashed, absorbed in the Lewesian magnificence!" Marian herself had scolded Bessie Parkes, now editing a feminist journal, for introducing her to someone as Miss Evans. She had renounced that name, she said, and did not want it applied to her ever again.

John Blackwood, who knew Liggins was an imposter, was at a loss as to how to reveal the real name of "George Eliot," for what was her real name? The ambiguity of her multiple identities—Marian Evans, Marian Evans Lewes, George Eliot—called attention to her irregular status. She signed her letters to him "M. E. Lewes." Finally, on June 30, Lewes wrote to Charles Bray, who with Sara and Cara had just been to Holly Lodge to lunch, explaining that he and Marian had decided to give up the secret—not least because Herbert Spencer had revealed it to the entire Garrick Club. He signed himself "The husband of George Eliot."

It is hard not to assume that Marian was embarrassed by her irregular social status. Barbara Bodichon, in London for a visit, brought the news to Marian and Lewes that the literary gossip in the clubs and drawing rooms of London had guessed the secret—Marian Lewes had written *Adam Bede* and kept her name secret because her notorious reputation might harm sales.

The controversy peaked when the literary and artistic weekly *The Athenaeum* wrote tartly in its Weekly Gossip column on July 2, 1859, that it was time to end "this pother about the authorship of *Adam Bede*. The writer is in no sense 'a great unknown'; the tale, if bright in parts, and such as a clever woman with an observant eye and unschooled moral nature might have written, has no great quality of any kind." It concluded that the author was "a rather strong-minded lady, blessed with abundance of showy sentiment and a profusion of pious words" and, moreover, that no woman of genius ever condescended to such a trick on the reading public. Savage as it was, the *Athenaeum* attack served to quash the Liggins myth.

In retrospect, it is curious that both Marian and Lewes clung to the pseudonym for so long. Marian's anxiety no doubt played a part; Lewes had known how insecure she was and that a false name protected her private self. In not telling their closest friends, however, their pretense verged on a *folie à deux*. But there was one thing neither of them doubted: their devotion to each other was unshakable. Marian inscribed the fly-leaf when she got the manuscript of *Adam Bede* (bound in red leather) back from Blackwood's, "To my dear husband, George Henry Lewes, I give this M.S. of a work which would never have been written but for the happiness which his love has conferred on my life. Marian Lewes March 23, 1859."

It was to be the first of many such tributes.

## Chapter Nine

# FINDING GOLD (1859–1863)

THE NEW NOVEL began as "Maggie" or sometimes "Sister Maggie," taken from the name of Marian's heroine, Maggie Tulliver. Lewes favored "The House of Tulliver," but John Blackwood won out with his own choice, *The Mill on the Floss*—not surprising, as he had offered £2,000 for it, more than twice what Marian had been paid for *Adam Bede*. Smith, Elder & Co., the London publisher of Charlotte Brontë, offered more than double the amount Blackwood did, but Marian chose to remain with her supportive Edinburgh publisher.

She was prosperous now that her work was a recognized brand, and she wanted the rewards that went with it. She rejected Blackwood's suggestion that the new book be serialized in his magazine. With sales of *Adam Bede* at nearly fifteen thousand, the once shy author told Blackwood that since there was now such a large and enthusiastic audience for her work, the new novel was guaranteed to sell well, and they would profit more from book sales than from serialization. However, she knew Blackwood was concerned that the straitlaced Charles Mudie, owner of the circulating library, might boycott the book, considering what was now known of its immoral author.

Still determined to write from reality, for *The Mill on the Floss* Marian needed to find an actual mill and tidal river capable of the disastrous flood planned to provide the climax of the novel. She and Lewes went first to Dorset, then to Lincolnshire, where they found the right model at Gainsborough on a tributary of the River Trent.

For the brother-sister relationship at the heart of the book, Marian needed no model. As Lewes reported to Blackwood, "Mrs. Lewes is getting her eyes redder and swollener every morning as she lives through her tragic story. But there is such a strain of poetry to relieve the tragedy that the more she cries, and the readers cry, the better say I." Recording a love that had been so close, then gone for ever, she wrote of a plain, bookish little wench who idolized her handsome older brother, who adored fishing with him in the Round Pond, and who was miserable when he was sent away to school.

The novel shows the author's mature intellectuality and confident philosophy of life as well as her determination to use the memories of her childhood as a creative storehouse. It has strong Darwinian touches (*On the Origin of Species* was published the previous year) as the younger generation struggles to distinguish itself from the old. It also emphasizes landscape as a contributor to personality. The river Floss is indeed a character in the story. In the book's opening, Maggie, the narrator, returning to the scene of her childhood at Dorlcote Mill, marvels, "How lovely the little river is, with its dark, changing wavelets! It seems to me like a living companion while I wander along the bank and listen to its low, placid voice."

The novel's main characters (apart from the Floss) are Maggie Tulliver and her brother, Tom. He is well schooled but unimaginative. She is his temperamental opposite, well read, rebellious, and emotional, but she loves him deeply. Feeling rejected by him after a quarrel, she runs away to live with gypsies, but she is rescued by her father, Tulliver the miller, who says, in terms familiar from Marian Evans's childhood, "What 'ud father do without his little wench?" (The twelve-year-old Maggie, as Marian did in her own life, knows she is not her mother's favorite and suffers from brusque maternal efforts to tidy her straggling hair.)

Unfortunately, Tulliver goes bankrupt and loses his mill. But eventually, Tom becomes a successful trader and investor, which allows him to recover the mill, and he runs it after his father's death. He tries to maneuver the tall, dark-haired Maggie into a sensible marriage, but she falls deeply in love with the handsome, wealthy Stephen Guest, who, despite being engaged, shares Maggie's feelings. Maggie ends up with Stephen on a boating excursion that, whether by accident or design, appears to be an elopement; when at last they return home, Maggie is fatally marked as a fallen woman. Her brother lashes out at her: "You have disgraced us all. . . . I wash my hands of you for ever," and she takes refuge with her widowed mother.

When a violent flood breaks over the town, Maggie finds a small boat in which she bravely rows to rescue Tom from the mill where she knows he is trapped. He joins her but soon they find the boat overwhelmed by flotsam from a broken dock. In a magisterial scene of authorial wish-fulfillment, there is a moment of recognition and reconciliation. They are swept away by the flood, "living through again in one supreme moment the days when they had clasped their little hands in love and roamed the daisied fields together." This was the kind of resolution with her estranged brother that would elude Marian's reach until the last year of her life, and then only through letters.

ON July 1, 1859, Marian and Lewes went to Switzerland. Lewes had sent off the final chapters of his lengthy *Physiology of Common Life*, in which he raised the question of hereditary versus acquired characteristics and dealt with the issues of life and death, the same grand themes Marian was touching on in *The Mill on the Floss*. Lewes's intention was to go to Hofwyl to see his sons—Charlie, sixteen, Thornie, fourteen, and Bertie, thirteen, who had recently joined his older brothers at the school—and to visit art galleries. Marian, upset by the fuss about the authorship of *Adam Bede*, could not bear to be left behind in England. While Lewes went to the boys' school, she waited for him at the Schweizerhof in Lucerne.

By happy coincidence, Marian's good friends from Wandsworth, the Congreves, were also in Lucerne. To them she admitted her authorship of *Adam Bede*, fretting a good deal while Lewes was away, "thinking of the possibilities that might prevent him from coming."

At Hofwyl Lewes gave his boys the presents that he and Marian had chosen: a new watch for Charlie, a Swiss knife for Bertie, and for Thornie ten shillings and a novel. "Is it *Adam Bede?*" they cried to their father. It was. Lewes had told Blackwood that Paris was "in a fever about *Adam Bede*" and its fame had traveled to the boys' school. While he was there, Lewes explained the complicated family situation to the boys. To his surprise, they were not shocked but delighted that their father had taken up with the author of the new literary sensation. They understood that their mother accepted that she had been permanently replaced in their father's life, just as they knew she had new children and was effectively Mrs. Hunt.

A month later, Thornie Lewes wrote Marian an affectionate thank-you letter, saying he was beginning "a correspondence which is to be lasting." He addressed her as "Dear Mother" and signed himself "Your affectionate Son Thornton Arnott Lewes." In the future when he sent letters, he instructed her, he would mark the envelope "p.M. = pro Matre" if it were for her; otherwise it was for his father. From then on, to the boys she was Mother or Mutter, while Agnes remained Mamma.

Dickens, unsurprisingly, loved *Adam Bede* and on November 10, 1859, was invited to Holly Lodge. Lewes sent his sons news of the famous guest, whom he had known in his theater days: "Today we are going to have Charles Dickens to dinner. He is an intense admirer of your mother." He told his sons he expected "a very pleasant dinner, at which two such novelists will gobble and gabble!"

The purpose of the visit was Dickens's attempt to persuade Marian to publish her next novel in his new weekly, *All the Year*

*Round*, on whatever terms she liked. She turned him down, however, because of the pressure of time.

In the autumn of 1859, Marian was still irritated by the rumblings of the Liggins myth. She was particularly annoyed that Charles Bracebridge, an Attleborough magistrate, was supporting Liggins. Bracebridge, using his local position, had made a personal crusade of discovering the originals of the characters in *Adam Bede*, interviewing people in and around Nuneaton who had known Marian Evans and her family. Marian wrote in a letter to Charles Bray that what infuriated her most of all was Bracebridge's reference to Robert Evans as a farmer:

> *Now my Father did not raise himself from being an artizan to be a farmer; he raised himself from being an artizan to be a man whose extensive knowledge in very varied practical departments made his services valued through several counties. He had large knowledge of building, of mines, of plantation, of various branches of valuation and measurement—of all that is essential to the management of large estates . . .*

As the ideas in Lewes's new book showed, he and Marian were in the avant-garde of scientific thinking. Back in London after their Swiss holiday, they started reading Charles Darwin's *On the Origin of Species* the morning after its publication on November 24, 1859. As Marian explained in a letter to Bray, "It is an elaborate exposition of the evidence in favour of the Development Theory, and so, makes an epoch."

The Leweses had already debated intelligent design with Sara Hennell. Many people then (as now) believed, for example, that the eye is too complex an organ to have evolved in stages, and that it therefore must have been created by a "designer." Sara had written a book, *Christianity and Infidelity*, setting out the arguments on both sides. But Marian had reservations:

> *I showed the passage on the eye, p.157, to Herbert Spencer and he agrees with us that you have not stated your idea so as to render it a logical argument against design.... I suppose you are aware that we all three hold the conception of creative design to be untenable. We only think that you have not made out a good case against it.*

In the spring of 1860, with *The Mill on the Floss* about to be published, in three volumes, Marian set out with Lewes for her first visit to Italy. She wished to escape reviews now that her identity was known. However, good news reached them in Rome: the lending library Mudie's had put aside its objections to her character and was "nibbling at a third thousand" of *Adam Bede*. A reprinting was underway.

Marian was disappointed with Rome. Unlike her first impressions of art and churches in northern Europe, where she had been dazzled by beauty, what she saw now left her unmoved. She particularly disliked "the ugly red drapes" hung in St. Peter's during Easter Week. From Rome the couple went on to Naples, Pompeii, and Sicily, then took a steamer for Leghorn on the way to Florence.

In Florence they met Thomas Trollope, brother of the novelist Anthony Trollope, who lived with his first wife in the Villino Trollope. While there, they learned that sales of *The Mill on the Floss* had exceeded six thousand and that the *Times* had pronounced, "George Eliot is as great as ever." Blackwood, Lewes, and Marian herself had feared that the new novel lacked the power of *Adam Bede*, but *The Mill on the Floss* was on its way to earning nearly £4,000 that year alone, a figure that would approach $400,000 today.

In Florence, Lewes made a suggestion for which future lovers of George Eliot's work would not thank him. For her next subject, he proffered the fifteenth-century Dominican friar Girolamo Savonarola, a forerunner of the Reformation, who preached against the moral and artistic corruption of Florence after the expulsion of the ruling Medici family in 1494. Savonarola tried to lead Florence in a purifying, book-burning revolution, but his influence was undermined by the hostility of Pope Alexander VI, and he was executed as a heretic in 1498.

Lewes thought the Savonarola story would strike a chord similar to Marian's love for the historical novels of Sir Walter Scott. His hope was to give her more distance from her story, saving her the emotional upheavals that *The Mill on the Floss* had cost her. As with all his suggestions, she grasped it eagerly: the research would give a point to their travels. They began reading intensively and managed to fit Savonarola's birthplace, Ferrara, into their itinerary.

After Venice, they went on to Berne, where, in June 1860, six years after she had begun living with their father, the Lewes boys were introduced to their "Mutter" for the first time. The meeting was a happy one, and it was decided that the oldest son, Charlie, quieter and more disciplined than his brothers, would come to live with them in London to start his career in the Civil Service, of which the post office was a part. Lewes apparently had agreed to take his three boys off Agnes's hands, leaving her free to bring up her younger children by Thornton Hunt. The middle boy, Thornie, who was named when Hunt was Lewes's best friend and coeditor, would finish his education at Edinburgh High School, where the Blackwoods would keep a friendly eye on him, while Bertie, the youngest and least able, would remain at Hofwyl.

Back at Holly Lodge, while studying the historical background for *Romola*, as the Savonarola book was to be called, Marian began a new novel, *Silas Marner*. In September 1860, she and Lewes moved to Harewood Square in Marylebone, nearer to Charlie's workplace. Marian had been itching to leave the Wandsworth house they had hastily moved into only the year before, where she felt eyes all around her. She wanted somewhere with shade and grass, but Lewes was insistent that Charlie get a good start on his career, so she agreed to move to central London—a sign that her career was not the prime concern in her life with Lewes. If she had been apprehensive about becoming a stepmother or losing the privacy she and Lewes had long enjoyed, she was soon reassured. Charlie was an excellent pianist and she played Beethoven piano duets with him in the evening on their Broadwood grand piano. She soon decided he was "the most entirely lovable human animal of seventeen and a half, that I ever met with or heard of."

Charlie began work as a supplementary clerk at the general post office—an appointment secured with some assistance from Anthony Trollope, who had worked for the post office for many years. Lewes had consulted him about helping Charlie get a start in the Civil Service.

A few months later when their Harewood Square lease expired, the Leweses shifted nearby to 16 Blandford Square. Frequent changes of address did not disturb Marian's writing. Within five months of its start, the complicated *Romola* having been put to one side, *Silas Marner: The Weaver of Raveloe* was on its way to Blackwood's for publication in April 1861. Also on its way to Edinburgh was a portrait of George Eliot by the artist Samuel Laurence. Done after nine sittings, the picture, while not unpleasing to the casual observer, so offended Lewes with what he saw as its melancholy expression that he demanded it remain in Laurence's studio. He relented only so far as to concede that Blackwood, who bought it, could hang it in the recesses of his Edinburgh office.

Drawing once again on her roots in what her new book described as "the rich central plain of what we are pleased to call Merry England," *Silas Marner* told the tale of a lonely linen weaver, an epileptic. Falsely accused in his youth of theft, Silas loves only his hoarded pile of gold coins. When a real thief steals them, his world seems to be destroyed, but he finds gold in another form: a golden-haired abandoned child whom he rescues, takes home, and rears, enjoying for the first time the warmth and joy of family life.

Marian traced the story's origin to a childhood memory of seeing a stooped linen weaver with a bag on his back. However, the story also drew on her own experience as a lonely outsider who suddenly tasted parental love, as well as conveying the shock of unexpected wealth.

The move into central London took its toll on Marian's health—or so she believed. It is difficult to discern what medicines she and Lewes were taking for their many and various complaints—or, for that matter, what these complaints actually were. Toward the end of 1860, Marian recorded in her journal feeling "physical weakness and mental depression," which she blamed on the London air, and she noted that she had taken "tonics." She was more specific in a letter to Barbara Bodichon about those who turned to religion for comfort. She did not need spiritual solace, she claimed. "The highest 'calling and election' is to do without opium and live through all our pain with conscious, clear-eyed endurance."[1] A milder remedy was lying in bed with wet towels on the head. Lewes, too, was often ill. One night he fainted and fell, hitting his head on the edge of the bath. The doctor who was called said unhelpfully that the cause was "debility" and found him otherwise sound in heart and lungs.

Every day that they were fit, the fragile couple walked in Regent's Park, talking about her Italian book. Marian tried out variations of the plot, reliant as always upon Lewes's reactions. In early February 1861, however, both felt so unwell that Lewes decided that they must go to the country. Such a short distance from London as Dorking in Surrey, less than an hour by train, would restore them—a cure assisted by hostelries with bucolic names such as the White Horse and the Barley Mow. Marian told Maria Congreve, "The wide sky, the non-London, makes a new creature of me in half an hour."

Her afflictions were not entirely psychosomatic. Nineteenth-century coal-fired London deserved its nickname, the Smoke. It was a foul-smelling place, with streets full of horse dung and rubbish. The air held a constant haze. Marian described it as the "fine dun-coloured fog." Dickens, on the opening page of *Bleak House*, evoked the filth of London: "As much mud in the streets, as if the waters had newly retired from the face of the earth.... Smoke lowering down from chimney-pots, making a soft black drizzle, with flakes of soot in it as big as full-grown snow-flakes.... Dogs indistinguishable in the mire.... Fog everywhere."

The Leweses, scientific rationalists though they were, believed that constant illness was the price they paid for having each other. Marian stated the equation clearly to her journal: "We have so much happiness in our love and uninterrupted companionship that we must accept our miserable bodies as our share of mortal ill."

In the spring of 1861, with *Silas Marner* due to come out, they set out once again for Italy. The reviews followed them, but Lewes, as was his custom, kept them from Marian. As usual, there was no need. The novel, George Eliot's shortest, was nostalgic, sentimental, and instantly popular. George Eliot was now being compared to Dickens. T. H. Huxley told Lewes it was a book "to do great good to people." Ironically, *Silas Marner*, which Marian had written to escape from *Romola*, was another money-spinner, quickly on its way to bringing her nearly £1,800 in the first year alone, roughly equivalent to $180,000 today. She could not turn off the tap of her earnings.

❧     ❧

LIKE many writers, Marian loved research and, panicking at the magnitude of the task she had set herself, simply did more.

Travel to Italy was essential for *Romola*, and the Leweses planned to spend two months there, from April to mid-June. However, arrangements required improvisation. Their route took them through southern France, where the railway ended at Toulon. With their new affluence, they could afford to hire private carriages to take them to Nice, then to Genoa and on to Pisa (Marian was sick twice during the drive), where they caught a train to Florence. There they were both laid low with headaches, sore throats, and fevers, all of which slowed down only slightly their visits to old libraries and monasteries. At one church they heard a blind priest give a passionate sermon pleading for a free and united Italy; Marian would draw on it for Savonarola's sermon in her new book.[2] Thomas Trollope, just returned from a visit to England, persuaded them to stay longer and visit the monasteries at Camaldoli and La Verna. At Camaldoli Trollope slept in the monastery but arranged, as Lewes's journal explains, "that I might sleep with Polly [Marian] in the cowhouse where the ladies are sent to sleep. . . . Capital beds; perfect cleanliness."

The Leweses returned via Berne and a visit to Bertie at Hofwyl. Back in London, poring over maps, studying the costumes of fifteenth-century Italy at the British Museum and learning their names—*sarco, gamuera berretta,* and *scarcella*—Marian began to write *Romola* in October 1861 following her usual formula of realistic detail combined with her perceptions of human nature and the human predicament. Lewes, who spent hours combing second-hand bookshops on her behalf, warned Marian against overloading herself. Depressed by the mountain of historical detail, convinced that she did not know enough, she considered the virtues of writing another English novel instead but pressed on. By mid-month, however, she was "utterly desponding" and almost gave it up.

She began again on New Year's Day 1862, but this book, unlike the others, did not pour from her fingers. Understandably overwhelmed by the complexities of her plot and the political and physical detail needed to reconstruct the period, Marian had stopped and restarted the book several times. She was working without her usual tools—local language and dialect. How could she know what words Florentines used to address each other in the 1490s? Thomas Trollope, who was visiting London from Florence, advised her that certain of her well-researched old Italian phrases were jarringly obsolete.

In January 1862, the publisher George Smith, of Smith, Elder, came to Blandford Square, ostensibly to ask Lewes about starting a new series of "Studies in Animal Life," following on from some already published in his literary weekly, the *Cornhill Magazine*. Smith, Elder had started the *Cornhill Magazine* in 1860 with Thackeray as editor and the serialization of novels was its specialty. At the same time, Smith asked whether George Eliot might be open to "a magnificent offer" for *Romola*. A month later he named his figure: a staggering £10,000. The price seemed a fair one for the privilege of wooing the renowned George Eliot away from Blackwood's. A further enticement was the proposal to illustrate the novel with woodcuts by the distinguished classical artist Frederic Leighton, who had been raised in Florence and knew its architectural styles well. The book would appear in installments in the *Cornhill Magazine*, something that, with the exception of *Scenes of Clerical Life*, Marian had not allowed with her previous books.

At first Marian held back. She confided to her journal on January 23 that "it is better for me not to be rich." She had written only sixty pages of the book and objected to seeing parts of it printed and meeting installment deadlines until she knew how the story was going to come out (unlike Dickens, who thrived on this method). But when Smith agreed to publish the novel in large chunks of forty-five pages or more, she agreed to let the *Cornhill Magazine* have *Romola* starting in July 1862, and cut her price to £7,000, roughly equivalent to $665,000 today. Even reduced, it was the largest sum ever paid for an English novel. Marian felt no pangs at deserting John Blackwood, who she felt had undervalued her work. She had read parts of *Romola* to Smith so that he would understand that he was getting no tale of Midlands countryfolk. He liked it, even so.

Smith's initial approach to Lewes had also been genuine. He thought Lewes was very clever and was thrilled when, in May, he accepted Smith's offer of £600 a year to serve as consulting editor for the *Cornhill Magazine*. Lewes was familiar with the young magazine, which had published his own work, as well as some of Robert Browning's and Tennyson's. The extra income, on top of what Marian was paid for the serialization of *Romola*, meant that Lewes would now be able to devote himself to his scientific writing—studies appreciated by scientists including Darwin and Huxley.

Blackwood was stunned to lose the author he had nurtured. He said he was not surprised at the Leweses' conduct. "The going over to the enemy without giving me any warning" stuck in his throat, he informed a friend on May 25, but he would not quarrel: "quarrels especially literary ones are vulgar."

*Romola* is set against the backdrop of upheaval and religious backlash following the death of the great patron of art, Lorenzo de' Medici, in 1492 and the expulsion of his family from Florence. The city was in a state of great excitement caused by the preaching of the monk Savonarola and the supporters of the ousted Medici. The philosopher Niccolò Machiavelli and King Charles VIII of France are worked into the plot, which centers on the pure-hearted Romola de' Bardi, the loving daughter of an old blind scholar. Romola falls in love with a beguiling young Greek, Tito Melema, who turns out to be a scoundrel; least of Tito's sins is his work as a double agent for the supporters both of the Medici and of Savonarola. He woos and wins Romola, but also goes through a mock marriage ceremony with a peasant girl called Tessa and has several children by her. Romola then loses faith in Savonarola, who abandons his prophetic mission to purge Florence of its Renaissance artists and scientists and return the Catholic Church to its mystical origins.

In the end, bereft of husband and political ideals, Romola devotes herself—like Janet in "Janet's Repentance" and Dinah in *Adam Bede*—to self-sacrifice and helping others, who, in this case, include Tessa's children by Tito.

*Romola* was and remains George Eliot's least popular novel. The autobiographical undertones of the plot, such as they were, escaped contemporary readers. Later readers, however, can see that the plot revolves around a man with two wives: one legal, and another who believes herself married to him. The story also portrays a childless woman who finds herself caring for her husband's offspring.

As it turned out, this difficult book took a long time to unfold. Seeing the early chapters in print before she had written the later ones added the risk that Marian might hear criticisms of her work in progress, and Lewes had to engage in his usual convolutions to prevent her seeing any word about her writing. She wrote in her journal, "I have a distrust in myself, in my work, in others' loving acceptance of it which robs my otherwise happy life of all joy." When Sara Hennell wrote criticizing the early installments of *Romola*, Lewes pretended to have lost part of the letter. Protecting Marian from any word about her books became a mutual obsession. Lewes was as convinced as she was that any word of criticism would stop her cold. "Excessive diffidence," he felt, had prevented her from writing for so many years. Now his principle, he told Sara, was never to tell her anything that other people said about her books, for good or evil.

On July 6, 1863, *Romola* was published in three volumes, with illustrations by the popular Leighton. Despite its relatively lukewarm reception, Marian, dazzled by her own scholarship, thought it was her best work. It was certainly her best paid. A month later, for £2,000, she and Lewes bought a long lease on a house called the Priory across the road from the west side of Regent's Park. Near the Grand Union Canal, it was an ideal home: secluded behind a high wall, away from main roads but within easy reach of the park, where they walked every day.

The Priory's attraction was scientific as well as scenic. Lewes was a member of the Zoological Society of London, which had its headquarters in the north of the park, and which had been a frequent destination in their daily walks from Blandford Square. But the most important feature of the Priory was its spaciousness.

The now-prosperous Lewes insisted that the house be furnished and decorated to his own high standards. He hired the prevailing star among London designers, Owen Jones, the architect who had supervised the decoration of the Crystal Palace in 1851 and whose 1856 book *The Grammar of Ornament* had urged greater use of color in British homes. What Lewes envisioned was his own exhibition space: a large, elegant salon whose centerpiece would be George Eliot.

*South Farm, Arbury. The birthplace of Mary Anne Evans. © Mary Evans Picture Library*

*Isaac Evans. Mary Anne Evan's father, a respected land agent. Courtesy of the George Eliot Fellowship*

*Robert Evans (1842).*
*Mary Ann's brother.*
*From* George Eliot's
Life as Related in Her
Letters and Journals
*by J. W. Cross*
*(Blackwood, 1885).*
*"Reproduced by*
*permission of*
*Warwickshire County*
*Council, Libraries and*
*Information Service"*

*Mary Ann Evans by*
*Caroline Bray*
*(1842). Now spelling*
*her name as Mary*
*Ann Evans, she*
*allowed her hair to*
*be curled for this*
*portrait by her*
*Coventry neighbor*
*Cara Bray.* ©
*National Portrait*
*Gallery, London*

*Sara Hennell, Mary Ann's trusted confidante, with whom she exchanged correspondence until the end of her life. Courtesy of the George Eliot Fellowship*

*Herbert Spencer by John Bagnold Burgess (1871–1872). © National Portrait Gallery, London*

*Mr. and Mrs. George Henry Lewes, with Thornton Leigh Hunt by William Makepeace Thackeray. Agnes Lewes plays the piano while her husband, George, and her lover, Thornton Hunt, watch. © National Portrait Gallery, London*

*John Chapman, charismatic owner of the* Westminster Review. *He brought Marian Evans to London as editor in 1850. Courtesy of the George Eliot Fellowship*

*George Eliot by François D'Albert-Durade (1849). This portrait of Marian Evans was painted in Geneva by her admiring landlord, Francois D'Albert-Durade. © National Portrait Gallery, London*

*George Henry Lewes by Elliot & Fry (1870s). Marian Evans's partner for twenty-five years until his death, he encouraged her to write fiction. © National Portrait Gallery, London*

*George Eliot by London Stereoscopic & Photographic Company, after Mayall sepia postcard print (1858). Marian disliked the way she looked in portraits so much she often denied that any had been taken. © National Portrait Gallery, London*

*George Eliot by Sir Frederic William Burton (1865). Marian Evans at age 45. © National Portrait Gallery, London*

*Holly Lodge on Wimbledon Park Road. Marian Evans lived here from February 1859 to September 1860, with rooms for Lewes' three sons*

*John Blackwood, whom Marian Evans described as "the best of publishers." Courtesy of the George Eliot Fellowship*

*John Cross, seated on the right. He was 39 when he married Marian Evans the year after Lewes' death and eight months before her own. © National Portrait Gallery, London*

*Ca' Giustinian, formerly Hotel Europa. Venice, Italy. Building from which John Cross jumped into the Grand Canal on June 16, 1880*

*George Eliot's grave, Highgate Cemetery*

*Drawing of George Eliot by Princess Louise on her concert program (1877). Courtesy of the Beinecke Rare Book and Manuscript Library, Yale University*

## Chapter Ten

# THE PRIORESS
# (1863–1869)

"MUCH TROUBLE ABOUT the two boys and much bother about the new house, continued happiness with the best of women," Lewes wrote in his diary on New Year's Day 1864. Three months earlier, his middle son, Thornie, having failed his examination for the Indian Civil Service, left for the colony of Natal, in southeast Africa, equipped with a first-rate rifle and revolver, a smattering of Dutch and Zulu, introductions to well-placed friends, and a subsidy from Lewes and his "Mutter." His departure coincided with Marian and Lewes's move to the Priory, where they gave Charlie, the eldest and most successful Lewes son, a party for his coming of age. The party was also a coming-out in society for Marian. She now had a home where she could receive her admirers.

Their designer, Owen Jones, took command of the decoration, paying particular attention to the drawing room. He insisted that all their old furniture be thrown away and replaced.

He designed the wallpaper, chose the carpet, framed the long windows with flowing drapes, and saw that the chairs were strategically placed around the numerous fireplaces. When the pictures were hung, he remained at the Priory until after midnight to make sure that every engraving—mainly Frederic Leighton's illustrations for *Romola*—was just where he wanted it. Lewes thought the result was exquisite—and the expense staggering.

But would the famous author complement the setting? To Lewes's satisfaction, Jones gave Marian a stern lecture on the neglect of her personal appearance; since her schooldays she had let herself appear as drab as she felt her face merited. For their first party at the Priory Lewes was pleased with her transformation and even made a note admiring the gray moiré dress she wore.

Up to this point, few women apart from Marian's close personal friends had visited her at home. Men, mainly acquaintances of Lewes's, had come often, but their wives stayed away. But with the splendid new home and the growing fame of George Eliot, the couple's social circle widened, and they shifted their mode of entertaining from Sunday evening soirées to Sunday afternoon "At Homes." Lady Amberley (who would become Bertrand Russell's mother) called with her husband, John, Viscount Amberley, and felt a sense of daring as she was presented to her infamous hostess: "Mrs. Lewes sat on the sofa by me and talking to me only in a low sweet voice; her face is repulsively ugly from the immense size of the chin, but when she smiles it lights up amazingly and she looks both good and loving and gentle." Their conversation, she said, ranged from the love poems of Elizabeth Barrett Browning to a book on the rape of wives.

Another guest conscious of entering an unconventional household was Harvard professor Charles Eliot Norton. Lewes had met Norton at Oxford and invited him to come and meet his wife, saying that she never made calls herself but was always at home on Sunday afternoons. After his visit, Norton sent a detailed report to a friend, explaining that "Mrs. Lewes was an object of great curiosity, not being received in general society." Norton knew the reason: "the common feeling that it will not do for society to condone so flagrant a breach as hers of a convention...on which morality greatly relies for support." He suspected that society was right.

Like many others brought into the presence of George Eliot, Norton was moved to physical description:

*The head and face are hardly as mobile as George Sand's, but the lines are almost as strong and masculine, the cheeks are almost as heavy, and the hair is dressed in a similar style, but the eyes are not so deep and there is less suggestion of possible beauty and possible sensuality in the general contour and in the expression. Indeed one rarely sees a plainer woman; dull complexion, dull eye, heavy features. For the greater part of two or three hours she and I talked together with little intermission. Her talk was by no means brilliant...the talk of a person of strong mind who had thought much and who felt deeply....Her manner was too intense, she leans over to you till her face is close to yours, and speaks in very low and eager tones.*

However, the professor also brought his wife, who, lacking English social prejudices, came again with her two children and invited the Leweses to lunch at their home in Kensington. Both

Norton and his wife came away with a strong impression of "Mrs. Lewes's" warm relations with her husband and his family, and of her good sense as well as her goodness.

Despite persistent poor health, in May and June 1864 the Leweses again went to Italy—Marian's third visit—and were accompanied, at their request, by the painter Frederic Burton. Despite Lewes's frequent illness and loss of weight, it was a stimulating trip for Burton, who was seeing Italy for the first time. He found it even more beautiful than he had imagined and delighted his companions with his extensive knowledge of painting and history.

At the Scuola di San Rocco in Venice, Marian was impressed by Titian's painting of the Annunciation, with its portrayal of an ordinary young girl who found herself chosen to fulfill a great destiny. As soon as they returned to London, she began a dramatic poem—the first she had attempted—to be called *The Spanish Gypsy*. Its subject was to be a young gypsy, "poor unwed Fedalma," who is suddenly called to lead her people in their fight against the Moors. Marian still had an appetite for historical Latin romance, despite her difficulty writing *Romola*.

When they returned home, the Leweses found that Charlie, who was twenty-one, had become engaged to Gertrude Hill, an attractive woman four years his senior. Although they wished he had waited until he was older, they were delighted by the news and held a celebration at the Priory. Marian wrote in August to Sara Hennell, her old friend and still her faithful correspondent, that she was concerned about Lewes's health: "He gets thinner and thinner. He is going to try what horseback will do, and I am looking forward to that with some hope." Riding, however, did not help; Lewes wrote that it "seemed to stir up my liver into unpleasant activity."

The couple never lost their faith in the healing powers of a change of scene. Neither was feeling well at the end of September 1864, so they went to Yorkshire, where they took the spa waters at Harrogate and admired the coast, the castles, and York Minster. They much preferred the minster to Peterborough Cathedral, which they saw on the way home. All the while, they immersed themselves in Spanish history and literature. Marian tried learning Spanish while Lewes brushed up on his by reading *Don Quixote*.

Back in London, while Marian struggled on with her first serious attempt at blank verse, Lewes left for Malvern to try the water cure and hill-walking. When he returned, saying he felt restored, he encouraged Marian's efforts with *The Spanish Gypsy*. It was then Marian's turn to fall ill. In December, she emerged from a week of "continual bilious headache." Perhaps, she guessed, she had "disordered" herself by taking tonics that disturbed the liver—"by trying to be better than Nature meant me to be." Even so, she was productive in her writing. By Christmas she had completed the third act of *The Spanish Gypsy*. Lewes was very pleased with it.

Marian had found Burton such a pleasant traveling companion in Italy that she now consented to sit for a portrait. She had always resisted photographs, for good reason. The camera was so unkind to her that she pretended the few photographs that had been taken of her, such as J. E. Mayall's of 1858, did not exist. When Harriet Beecher Stowe asked her for one, she lied: "I have no photograph of myself, having always avoided having one taken." For his part, when Lewes was asked for photographs of George Eliot, he would explain that "her shrinking from publicity has made her refuse all offers." But Burton's portrait, to be done in chalk, promised something softer and more acceptable. When Burton completed it the following year, Lewes liked it so much that—unlike the banished portrait by Samuel Laurence—he allowed the picture to be shown at the Royal Academy and thereafter hung it in his study.

Marian and Lewes had a happy first Christmas at the Priory in a group that included Lewes's aged and widowed mother, Mrs. Willim, a cousin, and Lewes's youngest son, Bertie. Lewes led charades and made an after-supper speech, and there was singing before and after the meal. In her end-of-year self-examination, Marian set down 1864 as an unfruitful year: "only three acts of a play and much illness."

Lewes was constantly busy between continuing his multivolume *Problems of Life and Mind* and editing the *Cornhill*. After two and a half years as consulting editor, in October 1864 he gave up the post and early the next year accepted an offer (which he had earlier declined) to edit the new *Fortnightly Review*. He also became an adviser to a new George Smith publication, the *Pall Mall Gazette*. Combining a wish to commission articles for the *Pall Mall Gazette* and a longing for a holiday, early in 1865 he and Marian visited Paris, where they went to the theater or a concert almost every night. As usual, she believed herself stronger for the change, so much stronger that, although she preferred to be alone with her husband in their "old tête-à-tête, of which I am so selfishly fond," they decided to hold their first evening party, on February 18.

It may have been a mistake. Four days after the party, Marian was ill again and in miserable spirits. Lewes, trying to reduce the stress that her work added to her sickness, kept her from writing, but despite his best efforts, a month later she was still under the weather. Her illness apparently had made her mercilessly critical of others. In a letter Maria Congreve, trying to account for remarks Marian had made about a third party, wrote, "When one is bilious, other people's complexions look yellow, and one of their eyes higher than the other—all the fault of one's own evil interior."

Several weeks later, in March, Charlie married Gertrude Hill, at the Unitarian Chapel on Rosslyn Hill in Hampstead, and moved out. Bertie no longer lived with them as he was learning farming in Warwickshire and Scotland. At the Priory, after an excess of what she called "Boydom," Marian and Lewes were alone at last.

It was the day after the wedding that Lewes abruptly changed his mind about the *Fortnightly Review*, brushing aside Marian's misgivings about his health and accepting the editorship. In a break with journalistic convention of the time, he insisted that all of the *Fortnightly Review*'s articles be signed. Its stance, Positivist and anti-orthodox, followed the Leweses' own beliefs in science, politics, and literature. Marian contributed two pieces signed George Eliot—one on rationalism in Europe and the other a book review of the well-illustrated 1868 edition of *The Grammar of Ornament*, by Owen Jones, their decorator.

Just as she had interrupted *Romola* to write *Silas Marner*, so Marian now set aside *The Spanish Gypsy* and began another English novel, once more choosing the Midlands setting that came so easily to her. The period suited her, too. *Felix Holt: The Radical* was set in 1831 in her fictionalized Warwickshire, "Loamshire," before the passage of the First Reform Act. Marian drew heavily on her memories of the violent riots between Radicals and Tories she had witnessed as a schoolgirl in Nuneaton, when the Riot Act had been read. As a result of the unrest, a detachment of Scots Greys was called in, one man was killed, and several others were trampled.

The opening pages of *Felix Holt* are powerful, perhaps reflecting Marian's buried longing for a son of her own, as well as an awareness of a mother's constant anxiety about a son in the far-off colonies. Mrs. Transome, "a tall, proud-looking woman, with abundant grey hair, dark eyes and eyebrows," sits in her drawing room in Transome Court, straining for the sound of carriage wheels upon gravel that will signal the return of her best-loved son after fifteen years in the Near East. The scene deserves a place among the passages in George Eliot's quiet fiction that can move the reader to tears:

> She sat still, quivering and listening; her lips became pale, her hands were cold and trembling. Was her son really coming? She was far beyond fifty; and since her early gladness in this best-loved boy, the harvests of her life had been scanty. Could it be that now—when her hair was grey, when sight had become one of the day's fatigues, when her young accomplishments seemed almost ludicrous, like the tone of her first harpsichord and the words of the songs long browned with age—she was going to reap an assured joy?

The plot Marian intended for the novel was fearfully ambitious, an interweaving of the political and the personal. Harry

Transome is, in fact, Mrs. Transome's illegitimate son by the family lawyer, Jermyn, who has been mismanaging the estate in Harry's absence. Not realizing the truth of his parentage, Harry returns, a plump and middle-aged Etonian, with a small son in tow, to claim his inheritance. He proceeds to scandalize his district by standing for Parliament, not, as expected, as a Conservative, but as a Radical. Jermyn agrees to serve as Transome's political agent.

In contrast to Transome, the tall, handsome, working-class-and-proud-of-it watchmaker Felix Holt sees himself as the true Radical because he wishes to educate the working classes, before changing the law to give them the vote.

Both men try to win the hand of the lovely, well-read Esther Lyon, daughter of the town's Independent cleric, the Reverend Rufus Lyon. As the novel proceeds, Esther learns that she is the true owner of the Transome estate and that her real surname is Bycliffe. Her supposed father, the Reverend Lyon, is in fact her stepfather who married her mother after she was widowed by a man named Bycliffe. It is revealed that Bycliffe, true heir to the Transome property, had exchanged identities with a fellow Englishman whom he found beside him when they were prisoners in France. The real Bycliffe dies and the assumed Bycliffe returns to England, where eventually the facts are revealed.

Once the truth of her legal identity is spelled out to Esther, she moves into Transome Court and begins to enjoy the life of a gentlewoman. She receives a proposal of marriage from Harry Transome, who has lost his election and who realizes that as she, not he, is the heir to the estate, the status quo could be preserved if he married her. Late in the novel comes the election riot, in which a policeman dies. Felix Holt is arrested, falsely accused of inciting the mob and causing the fatal assault, and imprisoned awaiting trial. In the courtroom Esther makes her way to the witness box and speaks of Holt's goodness. Although he is found guilty of manslaughter, her speech inspires the local men to petition the Home Secretary. The petition succeeds and Holt is released.

Which man will Esther choose? She wishes neither to marry Transome nor to be rich. She turns down his proposal and renounces all claim to the Transome estate. "Could you share the life of a poor man, then, Esther?" asks Felix. She could. In the customary manner of Eliot heroines, Esther turns her back on social rank and chooses love as the better lot.

Despite the more familiar setting of *Felix Holt*, it was proving to be a difficult novel and by late summer Marian needed a break, so she and Lewes escaped briefly to Normandy and Brittany. Back in London once more, Marian spent the second half of 1865 on *Felix Holt*, but got no further than chapter 10. Understandably anxious about the new novel, she immersed herself in research. At the British Museum she read back issues of *The Times* from 1832–1833 and the *Annual Register* to learn more of the election riots and reactions to the 1832 Reform Act. But that was hardly enough. Her prose, while richly descriptive as ever, was weighed down by the legal intricacies of the plot. She needed a lawyer.

Her choice was Frederic Harrison, a clever young Chancery lawyer who was a friend of the Congreves and, like them, a Positivist. Harrison gladly helped her pursue accuracy in the complicated plot she wanted to weave—the inheritance of an estate for which there were rival claims, false surnames, and hidden paternity.

Harrison applied himself "with zest," he wrote her, humbly grateful for the privilege of reading a George Eliot novel before it was published. He sent her lengthy legal letters offering hypothetical resolutions, such as, "Esther might very well be the heiress of Transome the settlor if Bycliffe was his cousin." With an air of professional superiority, he also recommended that Mrs. Lewes avoid reading books on legal subjects for herself.

She plowed on, writing long paragraphs that would sometimes cover more than two printed pages without a paragraph break. By the start of 1866, she was so depressed that, as with *Romola*, she thought of giving up the book. At the end of January she and Lewes went to Tunbridge Wells in Kent in another attempt to improve Lewes's health. Her book was "growing slowly like a sickly child, because of my own ailments."

The laboriously plotted book was finished at last on May 31, 1866. Marian indulged herself with a long, discursive introduction, strongly expressing her nostalgia for pre-industrial England, "when the glory had not yet departed from the old coach-roads, the great roadside inns were still brilliant with well-placed tankards." But, as if a local coachman were telling it, she described what she saw as the present reality of Dissenting chapels, factories, and coal mines, and then worked in the history of the Transome family and its duplicitous lawyer.

But who would publish *Felix Holt*? Smith, Elder, having lost badly on *Romola*, rejected Lewes's request for £5,000 for the book. Marian felt guilty about the *Romola* losses and as a parting gift gave the firm the manuscript of that novel as well as the right to publish her short story "Brother Jacob" for free. Her old publisher, John Blackwood, was so delighted at the prospect of winning back George Eliot that he quickly met Lewes's high demand (£5,000 would be close to $500,000 today). The sum covered all foreign rights; American, French, and German editions were in prospect. Even though Blackwood knew he would not recover such a high advance, he loved the book; in fact, he thought it superior to *Adam Bede*. Lewes privately disagreed but thought it was nonetheless a noble book.

When Marian came to write her now-customary, loving inscription on the bound manuscript of *Felix Holt*, she combined two of her many names: "From George Eliot (otherwise Polly) to her dear Husband, this thirteenth year of their united life, in which the deepening sense of her own imperfectness has the consolation of their deepening love."

Another book finished, another trip. In June 1866, en route to Germany for the first time in eight years, Lewes's "dreadful" headache on departure was erased by a calm crossing. He and Marian went on to revisit some of their favorite spots of their elopement journey. ("You may imagine the memories!" Lewes wrote to his mother.) In Antwerp they again saw Rubens's works in the cathedral and museum; in Brussels they went to an open-air concert in a park. In Bavaria they attended a performance of the Oberammergau Passion of Christ play.[1] In Amsterdam, Marian looked for the Portuguese synagogue where Spinoza was nearly assassinated. It no longer existed, but there were three others. Observing the ritual at one (which was remarkable to her because, in contrast to other religious services she had seen, there were no women present), Marian described for Sara

Hennell the scene: "The chanting and the swaying about of the bodies—almost a wriggling—are not beautiful to the sense, but I fairly cried at witnessing this faint symbolism of a religion of sublime, far-off memories."

From Cologne they went up the Rhine to Coblenz, then to Schwalbach, which Lewes described as "Paradise." They stayed two weeks, dining in their own room at the hotel to avoid English tourists, whose stares Marian dreaded. They immersed themselves in the solitude of the woods or listened to the band on the promenade perform movements from Beethoven and Haydn symphonies.

It had been a successful trip. Unfortunately, any improvement in their health was lost during the rough crossing on their return journey, even though they had hung around Ostend waiting for a clear day before venturing on board the ferry home.

On June 15, 1866, Blackwood published *Felix Holt*, in three volumes. John Blackwood rejoiced to be publishing Marian's work again and wrote to his London manager that the book was "a perfect marvel." Critics liked the book. It had the smells and flavors of her earlier work, although the legal complexities were seen to weigh down the story. Sir Edward Bulwer Lytton, author of *The Last Days of Pompeii*, wrote to Blackwood of *Felix Holt* that "the interest is of high intellectual quality. Beyond the question of interest, it has the excellence of good writing."

In September, Lewes's son Bertie left England to join Thornie in Natal. Marian took up *The Spanish Gypsy* once more and Lewes resigned his editorship of the *Fortnightly Review*, effectively giving up journalism for scholarship. Marian was delighted, as she told Sara Hennell on November 22, the day she turned forty-seven:

> *I have been telling Mr. Lewes that it is my birthday, and at that news he smiled through the sad look of head-ache as he lay on his pillow. It is the second morning that he has been unable to get up to breakfast, from the presence of that horrible demon, who has taken possession of his poor body as a penalty for our entertainment of a gentlemen's party on Tuesday.... However, I am comparatively at ease now he has given up his editorship and has nearly finished his History.*

Always anxious about Lewes's frail health, Marian strongly identified with Queen Victoria's suffering after the loss of Prince Albert five years earlier. Indeed, she worried more about Lewes's illnesses than her own. Sometimes, in the midst of happiness, she found herself crying at "the thought of the parting that must come." What would she do without her George?

⊰⊱    ⊱⊰

MARIAN's dramatic poem was still in progress, and Spain was therefore the logical destination for their next trip. But could their health stand it? In a letter to an acquaintance who had offered to lend them a house, Marian listed the difficulties that frightened them, despite their longing to go: "the length of the journey, the terribly cold winds on the high lands of central Spain, and the nature of the Spanish cooking etc. Mr. Lewes would get cold in travelling from St. Sebastian to Madrid, and there would be an end of comfort, and a suggestion of oil and garlick in his food would cause him endless gastric miseries." The mere mention of mosquito nets, she said, had made him tremble. Until he was more robust, such a trip was out of the question.

Nevertheless, at the end of 1866, the pair decided to risk the journey. They spent so much time at railway stations en route to Spain that Marian found she knew the advertisements on the placards by heart. In Biarritz in January 1867, she reported to Maria Congreve that they were reading Auguste Comte's *Système de politique positive* to each other, taking turns with each volume. "My gratitude increases continually for the illumination Comte has contributed to my life."

Unhindered by too much "garlick," the Leweses spent three months in early 1867 wandering through Spain by coach, train, and boat—Saragossa, Barcelona, Malaga by steamer from Alicante, over the mountains to Granada, Cordoba, Seville, then Madrid. Back in London in late March, Marian warned Blackwood, who was curious for details of her new project: "It is—prepare your fortitude—it is—a poem." It was not a work likely to make money, but Lewes was urging her to finish it.

At the end of June they went to back Germany—"Again we take flight!"—where Marian wrote what amounted to a Positivist anthem, "O May I Join the Choir Invisible." However, she denied she was a Positivist, and the Congreves knew she was not a wholehearted believer in their religion of humanity. She donated about £5 a year but never joined the movement.

As a celebrity with money to spare, Marian was always wary of movements for social reform. In November 1867, at Blackwood's invitation, she began an essay for his magazine titled "Address to Working Men, by Felix Holt." Blending herself with her fictional Felix Holt, she expounded her belief that the First Reform Act had unleashed the mob. After the Second Reform Act, passed in July 1867, had widened the franchise and doubled the size of the electorate, she felt even more strongly that the uneducated masses were not ready for the ballot; their votes could be bought by any candidate who treated them to free beer. Preserving stability was, for Marian, most important.

The Second Reform Act had been passed with the word "man" changed to "person." This change was made at John Stuart Mill's instigation so the voting franchise might someday be extended to women, a movement Marian was not inclined to support—"an extremely doubtful good," she wrote to Sara Hennell. Although she recognized that "as a fact of mere zoological evolution, woman seems to me to have the worse share in existence," she believed that the "moral evolution," in the form of love, offset that poorer share. Love offered a basis for "a sublimer resignation in woman and a more regenerating tenderness in man."

She put it even more bluntly when discussing the campaign to admit women to higher education: "There is no subject on which I am more inclined to hold my peace and learn, than on the 'Women Question.'" She sent £50 "from the author of *Romola*" to Barbara Bodichon, who was working to establish Girton in Cambridge as the university's first women's college, but said she did not expect to see women admitted to university in her lifetime. Thus spoke a celebrity and a natural conservative.

In the summer of 1868, the Leweses found themselves once more in need "of exile and quiet." They prepared to set off yet again to Germany and Switzerland—their third visit together in three years—just as *The Spanish Gypsy* was published. Blackwood accused Marian of "fleeing away from the praise to come as usual." He thought the poem was wonderful. So did the *Times*, which praised it as "a great work" from "a true poet." The poem's magisterial opening captures Spain's commanding geographical position:

> 'Tis the warm South, where Europe spreads her lands
> Like fretted leaflets, breathing on the deep:
> Broad-breasted Spain, leaning with equal love
> (A calm earth-goddess crowned with corn and vines)
> On the Mid Sea that moans with memories,
> And on the untravelled Ocean, whose vast tides
> Pant dumbly passionate with dreams of youth.

Far from praise and possible criticism alike, at Petersthal in the Black Forest, Lewes described their routine with scientific precision: They rose at six, drank the waters and walked until seven, had breakfast in the open air, read William Morris's just-published *Earthly Paradise*, and, after a light supper and another "ramble" in the woods, went to bed at nine. There *The Spectator*'s review of the poem reached them: "George Eliot surpasses not merely all women, but most men of genius."

Lewes had been to Germany on his own at the end of 1867, pursuing his studies in embryology and brain disease. At Petersthal, he was flattered when a very pretty girl, the daughter of an Austrian diplomat, asked him if he were any relation to the Mr. Lewes who wrote *The Life of Goethe*. He revealed his identity but asked her to keep it to herself. Swiftly, however, the news spread through the town that the biographer of Goethe was among them—by this time, the book had sold fifteen thousand copies and Lewes's name was well known in the German-speaking world. Two days later, at the end of Lewes's stay, the landlord of their hotel and all the guests assembled to see him off, bowing and waving handkerchiefs.

At Freiburg with Marian, Lewes was glad to see that she was celebrated, too. From there, they traveled four hours by carriage to St. Märgen in the Upper Black Forest, where Marian spent much of her time in bed to escape the cold. Back at Freiburg, the couple looked at Holbeins, and Lewes saw an embryological research scientist as part of his physiological enquiries.

They returned to London to find *The Spanish Gypsy* had sold well but that sales were now slowing. The reviews overall had been good; some carping criticism about anachronistic language was outweighed by *The Spectator*'s rave that it was "undoubtedly the greatest poem of any wide scope and on a plan of any magnifitude, which has ever proceeded from a woman." Marian told Blackwood she was interested in sales figures only insofar as good sales meant wide distribution. For their part, she said, she and Lewes were both happily free to write and study what they chose.

At the start of 1869, the year Marian would turn fifty, she and Lewes learned that his middle son, Thornie, was ill at the farm in Natal. Lewes immediately sent £250 and advised him to come straight home, knowing all the while that weeks would pass before Thornie received the letter. Meanwhile, there was some good news: American sales of *The Spanish*

*Gypsy* had reached 8,300—more than twice the number sold in England.

Marian's New Year's resolutions for 1869 were specific: to write some short poems, a long one on Timoleon, the champion of Greece against Carthage in 344 B.C., and a novel on marriage, which she had been contemplating for years.

## Chapter Eleven

# MASTERPIECE
# (1869–1872)

SOCIAL OSTRACISM LARGELY forgotten, invitations to Sunday afternoon receptions at the Priory were much sought after. Dickens joked to Lewes in the spring of 1870, "I hope to attend service at the Priory," and Darwin came at least once to the large Sunday lunch parties that sometimes preceded the "At Homes." The poets Alfred Tennyson and Robert Browning, the scientist T. H. Huxley, and the constitutionalist Walter Bagehot were also among the visitors, as were titled people and even clerics such as the Dean of Westminster, Arthur Stanley, who assumed the Leweses had married abroad. A regular visitor was Thomas Woolmer, the sculptor who had referred to Marian as a "_____" when she went to Germany with Lewes in 1854. Another frequent guest was Emanuel Deutsch, a young German Jew and an expert on Asian cultures from the British Museum, with whom Marian discussed Jewish history, a subject that had long fascinated her.

Lewes made their Sunday afternoons swing. As happy talking to thirty people as to three, he orchestrated the presentations to the woman he privately called Polly. He knew what he was doing—making his Polly the center of a salon like George Sand's in Paris. Close friends such as Sara Hennell preferred to call during the week.

Accounts of receptions at the Priory were newsworthy. The *New York Tribune* on March 25, 1874, headed an article "George Eliot. One of Her Receptions. Face—Figure—Manner—Voice—Dress." American visitors certainly assumed the couple to be man and wife. After Lewes had dined with the visiting American philosopher Ralph Waldo Emerson and his wife, Mrs.Emerson related to her mother, "Mr. Lewes who wrote *The Life of Goethe* and married Miss Evans was there, and was skillful in telling stories." Lewes's narrative gift was widely admired. Even Henry James, who told his brother that he found Lewes "personally repulsive," agreed that he was clever and entertaining.

The sound of Lewes telling a story leaps from an entry in his diary. He wrote down (as if fearing he might forget it) an anecdote he had heard about a stuttering but imperturbable general who asked the lady he had taken down to dinner, "Who is that p-p-p-purple faced p-p-party?" "That purple faced party, sir, is my husband." "Your husband? I'm so g-g-glad, now you c-can tell me whether he is the same c-c-colour all over."

Though she was not inclined toward joking herself, Marian must have enjoyed such stories, for she spent a quarter of a century listening to her little man tell them.

As 1869 opened, Marian finished a poem about Boccaccio and two more short poems, "Agatha" and "How Lisa Loved the

King." In March, she and Lewes again traveled to Italy. She was preparing to begin a novel that had been in her mind for more than two years, since *Felix Holt* was finished—for her, a long gap. They stopped in Florence, took another look at Naples, then settled in Rome for several weeks. While there, they invited an Englishwoman, Mrs. William Cross, to call at their hotel. Lewes had met Mrs. Cross, a widow with ten children, at her home in Surrey in 1867 while walking with Herbert Spencer. Turning up now at the Hotel Minerva, Mrs. Cross was accompanied by her son John (or Johnnie), a tall, handsome young man of twenty-nine. He had been working in New York as a broker and was about to transfer to London. Meeting the famous author, he was struck (he later recalled) by the "low-earnest, deep musical tones of her voice, the fine brows, the abundant auburn-brown hair, the grey-blue eyes."

In gaining an audience, the Crosses were luckier than the elderly American poet Henry Wadsworth Longfellow. When he called on the American ambassador in Rome, Longfellow learned that the great George Eliot and her husband were coming to dinner and he begged for an invitation. But the Ambassador's wife had promised the Leweses that no one else would be asked and felt she could not break her word. When the Leweses learned whom they had missed, they were as disappointed as Longfellow had been, but another meeting proved impossible to arrange.

❧      ☙

SOON after the Leweses' return to London, Thornie Lewes, now twenty-five, arrived from Natal, two months earlier than expected. He was in a dreadful state, thin, ill, and prone to convulsions. Even forewarned, Marian was not prepared for what she saw. Charlie Lewes fainted when he saw his brother.

Now living in the Priory, Thornie needed constant care and, as a result of providing it, Marian lost the thread of the novel she had in mind. She poured her literary effort instead into the "Brother and Sister" sonnets, saying all that she had not said in *The Mill on the Floss* (where she had said a considerable amount) about her love for the brother who no longer spoke to her.

To treat his son, Lewes summoned the best doctor he knew: James Paget, surgeon to Queen Victoria, to whom Lewes had been introduced at a British Medical Association meeting at Oxford the previous year. Paget was only too happy to visit the Priory. He had told Lewes that George Eliot was "the greatest genius—male or female—that we could boast of." Yet all Paget could do for Thornie was prescribe morphine to ease the pain. Great as his reputation was, Paget missed the diagnosis: tuberculosis of the spine.

It was at that point in 1869, on a Sunday afternoon in May, that the young Henry James was brought to the Priory by two American women, relatives of Charles Eliot Norton, promising to introduce him to George Eliot. The visitors found Thornie lying stretched out on the dining-room floor, contorted in agony, with Marian trying to soothe him. James was "infinitely moved... to see so great a celebrity quite humanly and familiarly agitated." Lewes was not there, having gone to fetch some morphine. When he returned, James volunteered to take a message to Paget's house, saving Lewes another errand. Following the visit, James sent his father in America his immortal description of the famous face:

*magnificently ugly, deliciously hideous. She has a low forehead, a dull grey eye, a vast pendulous nose, a huge mouth, full of uneven teeth, and a chin and jaw-bone qui n'en finessent pas. . . . Now in this vast ugliness resides a most powerful beauty which, in a very few minutes steals forth and charms the mind so that you end as I ended, in falling in love with her. Yes, behold me literally in love with this great horse-faced blue-stocking.*

As the summer progressed, Thornie's condition worsened. His mother, Agnes, came to visit him, sitting with him at the Priory for two and a half hours while Marian was out. She probably came at other times but the visits are not recorded. Marian and Lewes employed a nurse to tend to him when they could not, and Marian's old friend Barbara Bodichon also came in twice a week to sit by his bedside.

Despite the constant anxiety of that summer, on August 2, 1869, Marian began what is generally held to be her masterpiece: *Middlemarch: A Study of Provincial Life.* She set it in the town of Middlemarch, Loamshire, at a time when surveyors were laying out a railway and when the imminent passage of the First Reform Act was creating the general feeling that things could not stay the same.

For the character of Tertius Lydgate, Marian drew liberally and literally on the struggles of her late brother-in-law, Dr. Edward Clarke, the son of a squire who had arrived in Nuneaton full of ambition but who rapidly ran into local hostility and debt. Lydgate comes to Middlemarch as a young doctor, the son of a baronet, wanting to raise the standards of his profession and to make scientific discoveries. He hopes to introduce a fever hospital that might, in time, develop into a medical school.

Marian plunged into researching medical training, yet in September she admitted in her journal: "I do not feel very confident that I can make anything satisfactory of *Middlemarch*." Lewes reread *Romola* and told her once more how good it was in an attempt to encourage her. But in spite of excursions and walking, nothing would shake her depression, and she wondered whether she could manage "one more resurrection from the pit of melancholy."

On October 19, 1869, heavily sedated, with Marian at his side, Thornie died. The loss hurt more than she expected: "he is gone and I can never make him feel my love any more." After Thornie's burial, in Highgate Cemetery, the Leweses retreated to the secluded Surrey countryside. The deep calm of the fields and woods worked as before, and they returned feeling very much restored.

⟡     ⟡

LEWES himself was increasingly unwell. Finding it hard to get over Thornie's death, he suffered prolonged headaches and one night fainted in bed before going to sleep. In March 1870, in their persistent pursuit of health (and of scientific contacts for Lewes), they left once more for Germany. Marian wrote to John Blackwood that the new novel was creeping on.

In Berlin they met Prince Frederick of Schleswig-Holstein, who had begged to be introduced, and attended a grand party where Marian was "surrounded by adoring women, and a crowd of others all waiting their turn," as Lewes wrote to his mother. They went to hear Bismarck speak at the Reichstag, and on their visit to Vienna they were shepherded by their friend Robert (soon to be Lord) Lytton, attaché at the British Embassy. Marian caught a cold, which cost them their chance to see the emperor washing feet in the Maundy Thursday ceremony. After moving on to Munich, they returned to London in May, for once beginning to feel that they had, in Marian's words, had "enough of wandering to and fro upon the earth." The trip had been worth it, however; she told her friend Emilia (Mrs. Mark) Pattison that despite her constant illness Mr. Lewes had had "much edification from lunatic asylums and laboratories" they had visited.

On May 25 Marian went with Lewes to see the Pattisons; it was her first visit to Oxford, where Mark Pattison was rector of Lincoln College. At the dinner table was Mary Arnold (the future novelist Mrs. Humphry Ward), granddaughter of Thomas Arnold, of Rugby School. Carefully observing George Eliot from across the table at dinner, Miss Arnold was disappointed to see that she talked very little and was focused entirely on Lewes. Like many others, Miss Arnold took an immediate dislike to Lewes.

In May, Blackwood visited the Priory and for the first time heard Marian's account of her new book. She was full of doubt, as always, but he returned to Edinburgh convinced that the work in progress would be "something wonderful—English provincial life." By November, however, she had put aside the Lydgate story and begun another about a Miss Brooke, drawing on the theme of difficult marriage she had long had in mind.

The Leweses spent the intervening summer months traveling within England. In June, they went north for six weeks to Cromer in Norfolk, then to Harrogate in Yorkshire, where Lewes hoped to improve his health with the mineral waters. Next, they traveled to Whitby, where they were joined by a new friend, Georgiana Burne-Jones, wife of the pre-Raphaelite painter Edward Burne-Jones, who had recently begun an affair. The latest of George Eliot's female adorers, Georgiana thanked Marian after the visit for the privilege of having been allowed to unburden herself and to receive advice about her troubled marriage. Prevented from visiting Germany owing to the Franco-Prussian war, the Leweses then took themselves instead to Limpsfield in Surrey—"our favourite retreat"—where they walked and read aloud from books, including two volumes of J. A. Froude's *History of England*. There Marian wrote the greater part of "Armgart," a poem about an opera singer who loses her voice—a fitting theme for a writer who was struggling desperately with her latest project.

Back in London for the autumn, the Leweses frequently went to concerts, usually "Pop Concerts" at the new St. James's Hall, designed by their friend and former decorator Owen Jones. Their Sunday receptions continued, less frequent but larger, and the majority of their guests came in the hope of a few words with George Eliot alone. Her first biographer, John Cross, recorded the scene:

> When the drawing-room door opened, a first glance revealed her always in the same low-armchair on the left hand side of the fire. On entering, a visitor's eye was at once arrested by the massive head. The abundant hair, streaked with grey now, was

draped with lace, arranged mantilla-fashion, coming to a point at the top of the forehead. If she were engaged in conversation, her body was usually bent forward with eager, anxious desire to get as close as possible to the person with whom she talked. She had a great dislike to raising her voice, and often became so wholly absorbed in conversation, that the announcement of an incoming visitor sometimes failed to attract her attention...the moment they recognised a friend, they smiled a rare welcome— sincere, cordial, grave—straight from the heart.

IN 1870, shortly after her fifty-first birthday, Marian changed her plan for the new novel. She decided that she would combine the story of Miss Brooke with that of Tertius Lydgate. The resulting book, still to be called *Middlemarch,* would be written in eight parts and would now tell of two disastrous marriages. And yet by year's end Marian had written only a hundred pages of "Miss Brooke." In her ritual end-of-year entry into her journal (written on the Isle of Wight, where they spent Christmas), she summed up 1870: "In my private lot I am unspeakably happy, loving and beloved. But I am doing little for others."

Progress with *Middlemarch* continued slowly. By mid-March 1871, Marian complained in her journal, "It is grievous to me how little...I manage to get done." Yet by the beginning of June, Blackwood held the first part of *Middlemarch* in his hands and pronounced himself "intensely delighted with Miss Brooke." He expected she would repeat, if not excel, her previous triumphs. When he read the second part a month later, he worried that it introduced completely new characters, but added, as "you beau-tifully express it, we never know who are to influence our lives."

For the summer of 1871 the Leweses went to Shottermill in Surrey for four months while the Priory was being extensively renovated. The drawing room was being enlarged by the removal of a wall; a new bathroom was being added. The couple was also keeping their eyes out for a suitable country house. Comfortably settled in the countryside, Marian backed out of an invitation she had accepted to go to Edinburgh for the Walter Scott Centenary in August. No extrovert, and supremely self-conscious, she could not face such a very public appearance. Blackwood was disap-pointed but suggested she had done well to escape the "forward vulgar monsters" who frequented that sort of gathering.

While at Shottermill, the Leweses became acquainted with Alfred Tennyson, poet laureate since 1850, who lived three miles away. Lewes mockingly referred to him as "one of the 'hill-folk' here" who had found them out and threatened to break the per-fection of their solitude, but he invited the poet to come to meet George Eliot. Tennyson did so, then returned home to tell his wife that the writer looked "like the picture of Savonarola."[1] Even so, the couples became friends, and at the end of the sum-mer, when both Tennysons came to call, the poet read his work, finishing, at Lewes's request, with "Guinevere." The reading, his wife noted, "made George Eliot weep."

Lewes liked to live well, as his expensive restoration of the Priory showed. Preparing for their return to London, he asked his son Charlie to place an order for three bottles of brandy, a half pound of coffee, and four pounds of tea to arrive the day of their homecoming.

Brandy was little help to Marian when she fell ill with an acute intestinal disturbance. She blamed this on the lingering smell of paint at the Priory, but the two doctors whom Lewes summoned thought the more likely cause was an infection of the colon. The attack, Marian told Cara Bray, had been sharper than anything she had had as a girl and had left her "thin as a mediaeval Christ." Lewes, she said, had been "housekeeper, secretary and Nurse all in one"—duties all the more essential as Grace and Amelia, sisters whom they employed as their trusted servants, had given notice. Marian saw the cause as the social differences between "our drawing-room point of view and that of the kitchen."

In October, the couple went to call on Mrs. Cross at her Surrey home in Weybridge, where they once more met her son Johnnie. The visit marked a momentous change in the Leweses' lives; recognizing the well-spoken young man as a capable banker, they asked him to manage their financial affairs. Marian, with her entrenched habit of creating family ties for herself to replace those she had lost through death and alienation, decided to consider Johnnie Cross their nephew, and from then on in her letters she addressed him as such.

In January 1872 a little book, *Wise, Witty and Tender Sayings*, subtitled *In Prose and Verse Selected from the Works of George Eliot*, was published. It was the work of Alexander Main, a young Scot who worshipped George Eliot as the Shakespeare of the novel, and was filled with snippets from her work up to and including *The Spanish Gypsy*. By presenting certain quotations as coming from George Eliot herself ("in propria persona"), the collection also reveals the author's habit of delivering in her fiction godlike pronouncements in her own voice. In "Janet's Repentance," for example, she states: "The first condition of human goodness is something to love; the second, something to reverence." One aphorism, taken from *Adam Bede*, was, "One can say everything best over a meal," and another, from *The Mill on the Floss*, "We are all apt to believe what the world believes about us."

Charming though it was, the appearance of *Sayings* was peripheral to the publication of the first book of *Middlemarch*. Marian was astonished by the novel's reception: "quite beyond my most daring hopes." The writer E. F. S. Pigott told Lewes, correctly, that it surpassed *Adam Bede* and *Romola*. To celebrate, the Leweses decided to give their first party in four years—"six to dine, and a small rush of people after dinner, for the sake of music." Lewes liked social life more than Marian did; she did not feel up to the demands of the London social season and looked forward to going to the country.

In May 1872, at Redhill in Surrey, working in "a swamp of illness," Marian completed the fifth book of *Middlemarch*, with three of her projected eight books as yet unfinished. The couple told no one their address. "Mrs. Lewes is visibly improving in health," Lewes told their new friend Alexander Main, "and writing, writing, writing—ye gods! How she is writing!"

Lewes was a vigilant guardian. When Marian was not feeling well, he prevented her from writing and took her outdoors. He warded off admirers, even such a distinguished one as Edward Dowden, a professor from Trinity College Dublin. When Dowden presumed to send George Eliot his article about her, Lewes responded coldly that it was "well known to all Mrs. Lewes's friends that she abstains on principle from reading what is written about her works."

With the fifth book of *Middlemarch* published in August 1872, the Leweses spent six weeks in Germany at Bad Homburg—a spa they chose for its waters, not for the gambling for which it was known, they assured their friends. There, in November, Marian brought her great novel to a close. It had been a strain writing for serialization, composing the story whose outcome she had not yet decided with the knowledge that her readers were hoping (in vain) that Dorothea and Lydgate would be married. At its conclusion, however, Marian wrote to Main that she was "thoroughly at peace about it—not because I am convinced of its perfections, but because I have lived to give out what it was in me to give." She inscribed the bound manuscript: "To my dear Husband, George Henry Lewes, in this nineteenth year of our blessed union."

But cold and dampness dogged them for most of their stay, and a cold train journey from Strasbourg to Paris added to their misery. "Don't you think that this planet is getting more uncomfortable than it used to be?" she asked Sara.

The Leweses returned to London in time for the publication of the final books of *Middlemarch* in December 1872. Marian had promised Blackwood there would be no tragic ending—an assurance he might have liked, for *The Spectator* had pronounced her "the most melancholy of authors." And she was true to her word.

*Middlemarch* is, above all, a novel of a tight community—a weblike world in which lives are connected in ways that the characters cannot see for themselves.

At the center of the first major plot is Miss Dorothea Brooke, or Dodo, an idealistic, ardent young woman with only an eccentric uncle to guide her. Dorothea is beautiful but afraid of adornment because she is religious and suspicious of vanity. She blunders into a marriage with a desiccated clerical pedant, Edward Casaubon. Their marriage founders on the honeymoon in Rome, where Dorothea is overwhelmed by the presence of ancient art and (as Marian had been) by the heavy red drapes at St. Peter's. Decorously avoiding a bedroom scene of attempted consummation, the author delicately conveys Casaubon's impotence by having him discover that his "stream of affection" is only "an exceedingly shallow rill."

Dorothea, looking for a role in life, still hopes that she can learn from her elderly husband by assisting him on his great work, *Key to All Mythologies*. He rejects her attempts to help, insisting on working alone. He then dies, having malevolently specified in his will that Dorothea forfeits all his wealth if she marries his young cousin, Will Ladislaw, an artist and a newcomer to Middlemarch, to whom Casaubon could see Dorothea was attracted.

The novel's other plot follows the young doctor, Tertius Lydgate, who, like Dorothea, makes a hopeless marriage. He allows himself to be trapped by the beautiful Rosamond Vincy, daughter of a ribbon manufacturer who is also the mayor of Middlemarch. Selfish, manipulative, and greedy, she thwarts Lydgate's idealistic hopes of making significant scientific discoveries and improving medical treatment in the town, a proposition that the Middlemarchers view as intrusive social change. Soon Lydgate falls into debt and has to borrow money from the mayor's wealthy brother-in-law, Bulstrode.

Dorothea, meanwhile, marries Ladislaw. Like so many of George Eliot's heroines, she abandons personal aspiration for love and dedicates herself to giving "wifely help" to her husband,

who becomes "an ardent public man"—a Member of Parliament
with great hopes for what will be achieved under reform (the
First Reform Act of 1832). Yet Dorothea's life is far from wasted:
the novel concludes that "the effect of her being on those around
her was incalculably diffusive: for the growing good of the world
is partly dependent on unhistoric acts."

Marian poured a lifetime of observation into her characters.
Not only fluent but also wise, she could confidently make judg-
ments about the relationship between Lydgate and Rosamond
who, as husband and wife, she said suffered from a "total missing of each other's mental track, which is too evidently possible even between persons who are continually thinking of each
other."

As a picture of the interwoven society that existed in the
England of the early nineteenth century, *Middlemarch* was written for people who read at leisure and for whom a novel of nine
hundred pages was a treat. As a pronouncement on the quiet sadness of life, it was inspirational. The scene of Dorothea in Rome,
sobbing bitterly at the dismal failure of her marriage, gave the
author an opportunity for a magisterial and often-quoted observation on the ordinariness of disappointment in life:

Some discouragement, some faintness of heart at the new real
future which replaces the imaginary, is not unusual, and we do
not expect people to be deeply moved by what is not unusual.
That element of tragedy which lies in the very fact of frequency,
has not yet wrought itself into the coarse emotion of mankind;
and perhaps our frames could hardly bear much of it. If we had
a keen vision and feeling of all ordinary human life, it would be

like hearing the grass grow and the squirrel's heart beat, and we should die of that roar which lies on the other side of silence. As it is, the quickest of us walk about well wadded with stupidity.

BLACKWOOD predicted that the publication of *Middlemarch* would be one of the landmarks of 1872. So it proved and its reputation has grown with time. In 1919, on the centennial of Eliot's birth, Virginia Woolf declared it "one of the few English novels written for grown-up people." In 1948 the Cambridge University critic F. R. Leavis called it the only book to represent George Eliot's mature genius and ranked it as one of the greatest works of English fiction. In 2007, the novelist A. S. Byatt hailed it as "anti-romantic, yet intensely passionate" and held it to be possibly the greatest English novel.

It was and remains the most talked-about of George Eliot's books and is placed high on lists of the world's favorite English novels. From the time of its publication, readers recognized passages in it that seemed to refer to their own lives. "I have been a Fred Vincy ever so long, only not so little ugly and not so little unintelligent," wrote a young man from California, thanking the author for *Middlemarch*. "You, who are a great lady," the fan continued, "may smile a moment at my folly which dares to love you for your goodness and inspiring hand-iwork." Charles Bray spotted himself in Mr. Brooke, a land-owner described as a "leaky minded fool" with intellectual pretensions, "miscellaneous opinions, acquiescent temper and uncertain vote."

At the time of the book's appearance, the critics were rapturous. The *Daily Telegraph* said it was "almost profane to speak of ordinary novels in the same breath as George Eliot's." The *Times* waited until March 1873 to publish its four-column review by Frederick Broome, who raved, "There are few novels in the language which will repay reading over again so well as *Middlemarch*."

Marian's old friend Herbert Spencer, a man not given to superlatives, told Lewes after reading Book VII, "I cannot conceive anything more perfectly done." Even the New England poet Emily Dickinson wrote to a cousin, "What do I think of *Middlemarch*? What do I think of glory?"

Even before the book had been published in full, the character of the rigid scholar Casaubon and his grandiose *Key to All Mythologies* had become cultural currency. In 1872 Marian's correspondent Harriet Beecher Stowe inquired whether Casaubon was modeled on George Henry Lewes, who she knew had written a sweeping history of philosophy "to solve and settle all things."

Far from taking offense, Marian was artist enough to see all of her characters as composites drawn from her own imagination, and she politely thanked Mrs. Stowe for helpful words:

> But do not for a moment imagine that Dorothea's marriage experience is drawn from my own. Impossible to conceive any creature less like Mr. Casaubon than my warm, enthusiastic husband, who cares much more for my doing than for his own.... I fear that the Casaubon tints are not quite foreign to my own mental complexion. At any rate I am very sorry for him.

She protested too much, however. Lewes's work-in-progress, uniting physics and philosophy and presenting a physiological basis for the mind, was as grandiose as Casaubon's. Indeed, he often drew the comparison himself. He told Blackwood, "The shadow of old Casaubon hangs over me and I fear my *Key to All Psychologies* will have to be left to Dorothea." Blackwood himself played along with the joke, referring to Lewes's book as the *Key to All Mythologies* when its actual title was *Problems of Life and Mind*. At the same time, Tertius Lydgate's desire to make scientific discoveries "through patient thought and the renunciation of small desires" seems clearly drawn from Lewes's personal involvement in the scientific debates of the time. He was an early contributor to the new scientific journal *Nature* (launched in November 1869), in which he elucidated in rationalistic, contemporary terms the statement of the eighteenth-century philosopher Kant that space was a "form of thought."

By December 21, Blackwood reported that the total sales of all eight books of *Middlemarch* had reached 22,431. The Leweses began seriously to hunt for a country house, with Johnnie Cross as their agent. As Marian wrote, "My dear Nephew, A thousand thanks for your kind interest in our project."

Spending Christmas with the Cross family at Weybridge, enjoying charades and carols, the Leweses were only sorry that the last two days of their visit were spoiled by Marian's ill health. It is notable that nothing else had marred their holiday; the secret of the Leweses' marital status had evidently emerged over the dinner-table conversation at Weybridge. Back in London,

Lewes wrote to Mrs. Cross, asking, "Did nephew Johnnie forgive his uncle and aunt at lunch yesterday when he 'found they were not'?"

Johnnie Cross did more than forgive them; he made himself indispensible.

## Chapter Twelve

# REACHING THE HEIGHTS (1872–1878)

MARIAN WAS DISGUSTED by the gamblers in Bad Homburg, the nineteenth-century gaming capital of Europe, when she traveled there in the autumn of 1872. She watched a lovely young woman whom she knew to be Byron's grandniece lose £500 in one sitting. The description of the casino scene she sent to Mrs. Cross makes one glad that George Eliot never saw Las Vegas:

> The sight of the dull faces bending round the gaming tables, the raking-up of the money, and the flinging of the coins towards the winners by the hard-faced croupiers, the hateful hideous women staring at the board like stupid monomaniacs—all this seems to me the most abject presentation of mortals grasping after something called a good that can be seen on the face of this little earth. Burglary is heroic compared with it.

The shudder of revulsion ignited another book, but one that was slow to catch fire.

Back in London for the spring of 1873, the Leweses had a busy social season, despite their continuing ailments. "Lords and Ladies, poets and cabinet ministers, artists and men of science, crowd upon us on Sundays," Marian wrote, though they tried to keep weekdays free for work.

In May they went to Cambridge, where they met the philosopher and psychic researcher F. W. H. Myers and other Trinity intellectuals, and watched a boat race. Next, they went to Oxford, where Marian impressed their friend Benjamin Jowett, Master of Balliol, as "the cleverest head I have ever known. . . . She talked charmingly, with a grace and beauty that I shall always remember. She gives the impression of great philosophical power." Her idea of existence, he judged, seemed to be doing good to others.

Having failed to find a country house where they might spend the summer, the Leweses traveled in June first to France, then to Germany, where the landscape was invigorating. Another motive for their trip was to investigate Jewish subjects for the new book Marian had in mind. Together they attended Friday night services at the Frankfurt synagogue, savoring the music and noticing how many of the congregation looked not Jewish but German. They accumulated books on Judaism, which they read aloud to each other, including a history of life in the ghetto. Back in London, both continued to study Judaism. Marian also enlisted the help of her Jewish friend Emanuel Deutsch, from the British Museum. A frequent guest at the Priory, Deutsch gave her weekly lessons in Hebrew, and she called him "Dear Rabbi."

When Deutsch became ill and depressed, she cautioned him against thoughts of suicide. She reminded him of Mary Wollstonecraft, who attempted suicide in 1795, soaking her garments so that she would sink when she leaped into the Thames, but, when rescued, was "glad that she had not put an end to herself." Friends gave him money to take leave and travel to the Middle East, and Marian thought the journey would give him the best possible chance of recovery.

The Leweses were growing increasingly dependent on Johnnie Cross. In April 1873, Lewes wrote to his "Delightful Nephew," asking him to sell some U.S. bonds and shift the money to whatever American investments he thought best. Cross was making money for them; half of Marian's income of nearly £5,000 in 1872 had come from American holdings in railways and public utilities.

Cross was also becoming a confidant as well as a financial adviser. In a long letter to him in October 1873, Marian discussed not money but religion. She told "My dear Nephew" that she held no antagonism toward it but sympathy. She liked "the delightful emotions of fellowship which come over me in religious assemblies." Nonbelievers might be "better members of society by a conformity, based on the recognised good in the public belief, than by a nonconformity which has nothing but negatives to utter." This statement, endorsing church attendance as an act of social cohesion, represents exactly what she had done as a girl to placate her father, and still did. She often went to church services at Christmas. Marian's essentially conservative view of the world was shown once again in an observation to Georgiana Burne-Jones: "the devotion of the common soldier to his leader (the sign for him of hard duty) is the type of all high devotedness, and is full of promise for other and better generations."

*Middlemarch* quickly earned £9,000 (a staggering $870,000 today), and with their comfortable income, at the end of 1873, after consultation with Johnnie Cross, the Leweses bought their own carriage—the very finest, a custom-made landau. It was not only conspicuous consumption but conspicuous convenience for two people so often ill. They accepted Mrs. Cross's invitation that year for another Christmas at Weybridge, where they were becoming almost part of the family.

Marian told Blackwood that she was "simmering towards another big book," one inspired by the shudder of revulsion she had felt toward the gamblers in Bad Homburg, but she feared that people had such a high opinion of *Middlemarch* that her next book would inevitably suffer by comparison.

The new book "simmered" during most of 1874, and Marian worked as hard, if not harder, on research for what would become *Daniel Deronda* than she had on *Romola*, dwelling, as she put it, "among the tombs, farther back than the times of the Medici." It would be her most ambitious novel so far: two intricate, interwoven plots, ultimately covering more than eight hundred printed pages, set nearer her own time than any of her previous books but outside the Midlands, and incorporating a Jewish story for which she suspected the English public had small appetite. As usual when she began a book, she was overwhelmed with despair.

DESPAIR was not Marian's only affliction during this time. In February 1874, she woke up early in the morning with a severe pain on her left side. It was her first attack of kidney stones, the disease that had laid low her father in 1836. The pain lasted for hours and returned two days later, followed by a slow recovery.

Marian also suffered from the adoration of fans. *Middlemarch* had enthroned her as a goddess with an extraordinary effect on women. "Dearest," wrote the wife of the American philosopher Charles Sanders Pierce, "You will not be bored by another love letter—a little one?"

Her most besotted female admirer was Edith Simcox, a clever scholar, socialist writer, and businesswoman. After reviewing *Middlemarch* in *The Academy*, admiring the way the drama was drawn from the inner life of the characters, she wrote to the author, seeking acquaintance. Invited to lunch at the Priory on December 9, 1872, she fell obsessively in love with the woman she addressed as Mrs. Lewes. A regular visitor to the Priory from then on, she began to call Marian "Mother," frequently kissing her on the lips, on the hands and, falling to her knees, on the feet. She befriended the Leweses' maid, Brett, so that she could learn more about her beloved. In an age unselfconscious about same-sex attraction, she made no attempt even in her later writings to conceal that Mrs. Lewes became "the love-passion of my life" and that she adored her "lover-wise."

With a lover's jealousy, Edith was irritated to see her beloved Marian growing closer to Johnnie Cross, and when she visited she always tried to arrive at the Priory before him. Marian accused her laughingly of wanting "to poison Johnnie's shirts."

Almost equally smitten was Elma Stuart, a widow. As she lived in Brittany, the romance was largely epistolary, and she sent Marian elaborate gifts, such as ornate wood carvings, gloves, blue slippers, and a cream-colored silk kerchief. Marian encouraged

Mrs. Stuart by referring to her as "my beloved daughter"—revealing once again her pent-up longing for a child.

Many gifts arrived anonymously at the Priory, including a New Year bouquet left on the doorstep, with an inscription asking that "God's blessing might ever abide with the immortal author of *Silas Marner*." Lewes was moved rather than annoyed by such veneration. "When I came down to breakfast the other day," Marian wrote Mrs. Stuart, "I found my husband's face radiant over your letter (ex officio he opens all my letters)." As he read it aloud to her, his voice choked with a "rising sob which made it almost impossible for him to utter the closing words."

Lewes welcomed the chorus of love as a possible antidote to Marian's morbid lack of self-esteem. She, too, recognized that she found security in adoration: on May 22, 1875, she wrote to Georgiana Burne-Jones, already a devotee, thanking her for words of affection: "I like not only to be loved, but also to be told that I am loved."

Growing used to acts of reverence toward the woman commonly held to be the greatest living English novelist, Lewes took to referring to Marian as "Madonna" and to the Priory as "this Religious house." Her London public knew where to get a glimpse of her. With Lewes, every Saturday afternoon, driven in their carriage, she attended Pop Concerts at St. James's Hall and could be seen marching down the aisle to her seat in the sofa stalls—an expensive indulgence at seven shillings six pence each. Such was the intensity of her fans' veneration of her that after one concert in 1878, when she thanked a young lady who had helped her with her cloak, she was cautioned, "If you speak to me I shall cry."

Marian's admirers included royalty. When Queen Victoria saw her and Lewes's names on a letter of condolence to Alice Helps on the death of her father, Arthur Helps, Clerk to the Privy Council, in 1875, she asked Alice if she might tear off the autographs and keep them. In March 1877 the queen's daughter, Princess Louise, made an excellent sketch of the famous author at a concert for the blind. It was a good likeness, showing an aquiline profile under a pointed cap, with a veil streaming from her large head.

The following year Victoria's oldest daughter, the Crown Princess of Germany, asked friends to invite the Leweses to a London party planned for her and the Crown Prince. Lewes described the occasion in his diary as "22 at dinner and a number of swells and celebrities afterwards." The Crown Prince and Princess spent much of the evening talking with Marian and were disappointed they hadn't been told when the Leweses were in Berlin. For her part, Marian found the Crown Prince "really like a grand-looking antique bust—cordial and simple in manners."

Overall, the roster of names of those with whom the Leweses lunched, dined, and shared a concert box was glittering: the Wagners, the Darwins, and lords galore, including Lord Houghton (the poet Richard Monckton Milnes, a leading member of London's literary intelligentsia)—a brilliant social life for the woman who once could not be invited to dinner.

In addition to their busy social life, Lewes was working on his own book. The fourth and final volume of *Problems of Life and Mind* was to be titled *The Study of Psychology*. But he ran into opposition from Blackwood. "My dear Lewes," Blackwood told his author in May 1873, "I am sorry to say your book grates upon me more than I expected." As a believer, Blackwood objected to the idea that the world would be a better place without religion. He suggested, in the friendliest terms possible, that Lewes might wish to seek another publisher. Lewes, unperturbed, found another, Trubner & Co., immediately.

Marian, too, was hard at work on her Jewish novel, *Daniel Deronda*. Her fascination with the history of the Jews dated from her girlhood attempt to draw up a chart of ecclesiastical history and, following that, to continue with her work on Strauss and Spinoza. Her interest was deepened by her friendship with Emanuel Deutsch, who saw Palestine as the national homeland for the Jews. The idea so intrigued Marian that she thought of traveling to the Middle East, although, unsurprisingly, neither she nor Lewes ever felt up to the arduous journey.

As she began writing, she learned that Deutsch, her inspiration, had died in May 1873 on a second visit to the Middle East. She worked his longing for a Jewish homeland into the character of the Jewish scholar Mordecai, through whom a scarcely disguised portrait of Deutsch emerges.

*Daniel Deronda* was the only novel George Eliot set in her own time period. It neatly resolved her conflict between English and foreign settings for her novels by intertwining both. The English plot used a London setting, including the parts "most inhabited by common Jews," as well as a southwestern region called— borrowing from Thomas Hardy—Wessex. Marian and Lewes made excursions to Wiltshire to get a sense of the countryside, and while in London they visited the Spanish and Portuguese synagogue in Bayswater to have a glimpse of Sephardic Jewish

culture. For the complicated legal questions of inheritance presented by her new plot, she again consulted Frederic Harrison,
who had helped so much with *Felix Holt*.

In May 1874, *The Legend of Jubal*, a collection of her poems,
was published, including what became the much-loved "O May
I Join the Choir Invisible," expressing how the lost life endures in
the mind of the living. This idea was in no way connected with
belief in spirits, however; in January 1874, Marian and Lewes
attended, with some diffidence, a séance given by Erasmus
Darwin, brother of Charles (who was there, with his family),
along with a professional medium and committed believers like
F. W. H. Myers. Lewes spoiled the mystical mood by making
jokes, and he and Marian left early in disgust.

With her fame growing beyond bounds, Marian felt posterity
looking over her shoulder. She wrote to Blackwood that something should be done toward "the reform of our national habits
in the matter of literary biography." "Is it not odious," she fumed
(perhaps with the recent biographies of Dickens and Thackeray
in mind), "that as soon as a man is dead his desk is raked, and
every insignificant memorandum, which he never meant for the
public, is printed for the gossiping amusement of people too idle
to re-read his books?"

Determined not to spend the summer in London, the Leweses
intensified their search for a country house. By June 1874, they
were lodged at Earlswood Common, near Redhill in Surrey,
from where Marian hoped to make good progress on her novel,
as she had been distracted by her health in recent months. Their
delight in the Surrey countryside—"prettier than half the places
one crosses the Channel to see"—was heightened by having

their own carriage to drive them about and also by having their Priory servants with them. Their good mood was helped by a letter from Blackwood in August, informing them that, in May and June 1874, *Middlemarch* had sold more than six thousand copies and another reprinting was underway. Marian thanked him for sending the good news: "The sale of *Middlemarch* is wonderful out of all whooping."

By mid-1875, Blackwood had still not seen any of *Daniel Deronda*. His nephew William, son of his brother William, who had died, visited the Leweses in London and tried to take the first part of the manuscript with him back to Edinburgh. The author's horror was so great, he told his uncle, that he felt as if he were trying to take away her baby. Blackwood himself, finally getting hold of the starting segment on a trip to London, read it in one sitting and congratulated her on "this most auspicious opening of another immortal work." Marian was almost as fortunate in her publisher, with his constancy and admiration, as she was in her life's partner.

While the Priory was being redecorated yet again in the summer of 1875, the Leweses made another summer retreat with their servants, this time west of London to Rickmansworth in Hertfordshire. There, news reached them from Natal that Lewes's youngest son, Bertie, had died. They had been aware that his health was poor. Out of the four sons born to Lewes and Agnes (one of whom had died in infancy), only Charlie now survived. Marian, with Darwinian reasoning, commented to Sara Hennell that all three boys had inherited "an untrustworthy physique" from their father. Eliza, Bertie's widow, was left with two children, Marian, age two, and George, just a month old. The news reached the Leweses in London with the painful slowness of mail at the time. Bertie had died on June 29, but the next letter his father and Marian had from Natal announced the birth of a son. News of Bertie's death did not arrive until mid-August. Charlie's impulse was to rush to Natal to bring back his brother's bereaved widow and her children, but as his own wife was expecting another child, Lewes convinced Charlie to stay. Lewes sent money instead.

Meanwhile, their adviser, Johnnie Cross, had been abroad for six months. When he returned in August, Marian was relieved and told her "Dearest Nephew": "What a comfort that you are at home again and well! The sense of your nearness had been so long missing to us that we had begun to take up with life as inevitably a little less cheerful than we remembered it to have been formerly, without thinking of restoration." She thanked him for a gift of a box and she promised to think of him whenever she opened it. As for herself, she wrote,

> *Of your unfortunate Aunt you must expect no good. She has been in a piteous state of debility in body and depression in mind. Her book seems to me so unlikely ever to be finished in a way that will make it worth giving to the world, that it is a kind of glass in which she beholds her infirmities.*

When the Leweses returned to the Priory on September 23, 1875, the abhorrent smell of fresh paint and the sight of unpapered walls drove them to take another holiday, this time to Shrewsbury, where they happened to find their surgeon, Sir James Paget, staying in the same hotel. When they returned to London two weeks later, however, the house was still unsettled. Marian's teeth, which had bothered her over the summer, were as painful as ever. She had two canines extracted under the influence of nitrous oxide, which her dentist was using for the first time. The gaps in her smile can only have accentuated her odd appearance.

Lewes, meanwhile, had been busy selling foreign rights to *Daniel Deronda*. Harper's in America, after a struggle, won rights for £1,700, and in Britain, Blackwood agreed on a flat royalty of 40 percent for each five-shilling part sold—the same that he had paid on *Middlemarch*. They agreed that *Daniel Deronda* would come out in eight monthly installments.

The last of George Eliot's novels, *Daniel Deronda* is insufficiently recognized as one of the best. Its heroine is Gwendolen Harleth (the author could hardly have chosen a name more suggestive of *harlot*), a slim, charming, overconfident young woman. Gwendolen is the daughter of a remarried mother who has four new daughters, lives in a stately Wessex home called Offendene, and expects Gwendolen to make a brilliant marriage.

In the novel's opening, the graceful Gwendolen is spotted by Daniel Deronda, a handsome young Englishman, at a German gaming table—a scene inspired by Marian's disgust at the gambling she witnessed in Bad Homburg. Returning to her hotel, Gwendolen is greeted by a letter from her mother calling her home, saying that they have been financially ruined.

Gwendolen decides to pawn her most salable possession—a turquoise necklace—at a Jewish pawnbroker's, and does so on an early morning walk that takes her past Deronda's hotel. Returning to her hotel, she is handed a packet containing the necklace and a note saying that the stranger who found it hopes that she will not risk losing it again. She realizes that Deronda must have seen her enter the shop, gone in himself immediately afterwards, and repurchased the necklace.

Deronda is drawn to Gwendolen but recognizes that he should not run after her. Her home in England is near his, on the Wessex estate of his uncle Mallinger. He meanwhile gets another chance to save a young woman—this time from drowning in the Thames. She is Mirah (Marian pronounced it "MYrah") Lapidoth, a young Jewish singer whose brother Mordecai, young, scholarly, and unwell, is a Jewish nationalist looking for a homeland for his people. Mirah is in despair because she has lost hope of finding her real mother and brother, whom she knows to be in England. Like Mary Wollstonecraft in 1795—of whom Marian had reminded Deutsch two years earlier—Mirah wets her cloak to make herself sink faster before she throws herself into the river. Like Wollstonecraft, she is rescued by a stranger—Deronda—who guides her to a lady who takes her in. (Marian and Lewes, scouting for a site for the drowning scene, chose Kew Bridge.)

Gwendolen, meanwhile, has no alternative but to marry her admirer, Henleigh Grandcourt, to save her mother and sisters from penury and herself from the fate of becoming a governess. Grandcourt is a balding, promiscuous, irresponsible aristocrat who has his own Wessex estate but is also (no wonder Marian needed legal advice) the presumptive heir of Mallinger's stately home, Topping Abbey.

The marriage is unhappy; Grandcourt humiliates Gwendolen with reminders of the children he has had by his mistress. Gwendolen herself is attracted to their handsome neighbor, Deronda. But how to get rid of an unwanted husband in a land of no divorce? On a holiday to Genoa, when Grandcourt slips off their boat, he begs Gwendolen to throw him a rope. She hesitates to the point where he is lost. He drowns and she is free.

Gwendolen confesses her guilt to Deronda, whom she sees as a spiritual adviser, but he cannot help her. Only late in the book does Daniel Deronda learn what is obvious to today's reader from the start: he himself is a Jew. His mother summons him from her deathbed and tells him the truth of his birth. When she was a young, promising singer, she married her cousin, who promised her that nothing would prevent her pursing her career as an artist. When she had a son, she gave the child away to one of her great admirers, Sir Hugo Mallinger, to be raised as an English gentleman and educated at Eton and Cambridge.[1] This revelation of his real identity makes it clear that Deronda must reject Gwendolen, follow his heart, and marry Mirah. No surprise, Mirah gives up her career, too, to be a wife and help Deronda, who dedicates his life to founding a Jewish national homeland—its location specified only as "the Near East."

The book is rich in passages showing the author's ability to convey the subtleties of sexual attraction. And yet such attraction is by no means a guarantee to happiness. The book ends with three women thwarted in their careers, two caught in "helpless subjection and an oppressive lot," and only the third, Mirah, married for love. It is odd that Marian, so successful in her own work and so happy with Lewes, should persist in picturing women caught between ambition and love and choosing to surrender ambition.

*Daniel Deronda* was finally finished in early June 1876, both Marian and Lewes weeping at Gwendolen and Deronda's parting. Sitting in her room, writing the final pages at a furious pace, she would not come downstairs even when Blackwood and his son came to the Priory for lunch. Yet Blackwood was more than happy with what he soon read: "Grand, glorious, and touching are too mild words for this last book." Lewes, however, was troubled to see his exhausted Polly "sitting pale and tired."

*Daniel Deronda* holds more contemporary interest than any of Marian's other books. When she wrote it, Jews had been allowed as Members of Parliament (by taking a Jewish rather than a Christian oath of allegiance) only since 1858. In 1868, Benjamin Disraeli had become Britain's first prime minister of Jewish parentage, a post he was to hold again from 1874 to 1880. The novel anticipated by twenty years the Zionist movement, with its impassioned plea for a Jewish homeland, and by just over forty years the Balfour Declaration, which indicated a British willingness to have a Jewish homeland in Palestine.

In addition to its broader political points, the novel also draws a vivid picture of Jews in Victorian London, as Deronda searches pawnshops around Hatton Garden, hoping to find a mother named Cohen with a son named Ezra who has lost a daughter named Mirah. When he succeeds in tracking down Mirah's father, the little children who emerge from the back of Ezra Cohen's pawnshop are described in terms that show Marian's evolutionary belief in transmission of racial characteristics. The baby is "a black-eyed little one, its head already well covered with black curls" who looks around "with even more than the usual intelligence of babies." There is also "a robust boy of six and a younger girl, both with black eyes and black-ringed hair—looking more Semitic than their parents, as the puppy lions show the spots of far-off progenitors."

The effect of such blackness in a blue-eyed society is reflected in a much later book, James Watson's *The Double Helix*, published in 1968. It describes the discomfort felt at King's College London in 1951 when the young DNA scientist, Rosalind Franklin, arrived. She never managed to mix in with the others in the laboratory. None of her King's colleagues realized that the London-born Franklin was Jewish or that "Franklin" was an anglicized form of Fraenkel. They all, however, noticed the dark eyes and the glowing skin and treated their "dark lady" as an adversary and a figure of fun. Seventy-five years after *Daniel Deronda* was published, "black eyes" still connoted oriental and alien qualities.

George Eliot's identification with Deronda is obvious. Was it because Marian Evans Lewes considered herself an outsider in English society? Deronda is described as being not religious yet "loath to part with long-sanctioned forms"; he suspects himself "of loving too well the losing causes of the world." In fact, the book's strong sympathy for the Jews led to a false rumor that still persists—that Lewes himself was Jewish.

On February 1, 1876, the first book of *Daniel Deronda* was published. To Blackwood's surprise (he was worried about the character of Mordecai), the public snapped it up; it looked as if it might surpass *Middlemarch*. Henry James described "the deep interest with which the reader settles down to George Eliot's widening narrative." But enthusiasm cooled later, when the Jewish plot emerged in Book II, with Mirah telling Deronda: "I am English-born. But I am a Jewess.... Do you despise me for it?" Blackwood told Lewes what he would not tell Marian directly: "Even her magic pen cannot at once make them [Jews] a popular element in a Novel."

The book done, on June 8, 1876, the Leweses left for France and Switzerland, the June heat having deterred them from going to the Maritime Alps. After a time spent in France, when both were ill with headache, diarrhea, and "Mutter's renal troubles (with blood!)," they moved on to Ragatz, a Swiss watering place east of Zurich known for its hot mineral baths. There they followed a disciplined routine: they rose at five or earlier, drank glasses of warm water, and walked until quarter to seven, when they breakfasted. After breakfast, they read until half past eight then walked for two and a half hours; following lunch they had baths. Lewes, after a recital of symptoms, asked his son Charlie to send Johnnie Cross word of their whereabouts.

They reached home in early September, "strengthened by our journey...but of course not cured of all our infirmities....Death is the only physician...that will cure us of age and the gathering fatigue of years." Waiting for them were four bound volumes of *Daniel Deronda* and a letter from the Chief Rabbi in London thanking George Eliot for her "faithful representation of the best traits of the Jewish character." Blackwood was surprised, having believed that it was almost impossible to make "a strong Jewish element popular in this country and it was perfectly marvelous to see how in your transitions you kept your public together." There were grumblings from "anti-Jews" and no sign that Disraeli had made any comment whatsoever, but the *Jewish Chronicle* in London welcomed the book, as did

Harriet Beecher Stowe in America, to whom Marian explained
the Jewish elements in *Deronda*:

> *The usual attitude of Christians towards Jews is—I hardly know*
> *whether to say more impious or more stupid...I therefore felt urged*
> *to treat Jews with such sympathy and understanding as my nature*
> *and knowledge could attain to. Moreover, not only towards the*
> *Jews, but towards all oriental peoples with whom we English come*
> *in contact, a spirit of arrogance and contemptuous dictatorialness is*
> *observable which has become a national disgrace to us.*

When David Kaufmann, a professor from a theological seminary in Budapest, wrote a favorable review in a learned journal and later made contact with her, Marian allowed herself to
acknowledge his praise directly. She thanked him for his "perfect response to the artist's intention":

> *Hardly, since I became an author, have I had a deeper satisfac-*
> *tion—I may say, a more heartfelt joy—than you have given me*
> *in your estimate of 'Daniel Deronda'...it is my rule, very strictly*
> *observed, not to read the criticisms on my writings. For years I have*
> *found this abstinence necessary to preserve me from that discourage-*
> *ment as an artist which ill-judged praise, no less than ill-judged*
> *blame, tends to produce in me.*

Her wish, she said, had been "to contribute something to the
ennobling of Judaism in the conception of the Christian community and in the consciousness of the Jewish community."

*Daniel Deronda* sold well in spite of criticism that it was
two books squeezed into one. In 1948, the Cambridge critic

F. R. Leavis savaged what he saw as the uninspired, fervid, and self-indulgent Zionist theme. He saw greatness in the magnificent portrait of Gwendolen, but "as for the bad part of Daniel Deronda," he wrote in *The Great Tradition*, "there is nothing to do but cut it away." The excision, he said, would leave a splendid novel called *Gwendolen Harleth* which, like Eliot's other best work, would have "a Tolstoyan depth and reality."

SUNDAY afternoons at the Priory grew quieter after the publication of *Daniel Deronda*—Eliot biographer Gordon Haight speculates that might be exactly what the Leweses intended. On one Sunday afternoon, Johnnie Cross was the only guest, and they talked about the country house they hoped he would find for them. And at last he did. On December 6, 1876, he secured for them a second home, for £4,950 (slightly below the asking price), the Heights at Witley in Surrey, an hour by train from London. Perhaps, the Leweses wondered, they should make a serious change in their life and "give up town." Reaching for another superlative, Marian described the two of them as "enraptured with this part of the country."

The Heights, redbrick with deep gables, was huge, room enough for servants and many guests, with four imposing chimneys and a long glass-paneled conservatory stretching along its front. It was surrounded by acres of wooded ground and garden and was handy for visiting the Crosses at Weybridge, not far away. In a jubilant mood, the Leweses spent Christmas with the Crosses once more.

In February 1877 Marian became severely ill. Lewes, who had himself been laid up for a month with rheumatic gout, pains in his ears, and nausea, heard violent screams from the drawing room. He rushed downstairs and found her hysterically screaming and sobbing—"not," he told his journal, "from pain but strange and excessive irritation in the kidneys." But, as before, once the affliction passed she resumed mildly active life, walking in the park and driving to northwest London, where she found the nearest approximation to countryside near the Priory. In March they held a party to hear Alfred Tennyson, the poet laureate, read "Maud" and "Northern Farmers." Marian was well enough to last the length of the evening, which did not break up until midnight.

In June 1877 the Leweses moved into the Heights, where they found themselves plagued with the plumbing and decorating problems they both loathed. Hardly any of their furniture had arrived and Marian was loath to purchase new furnishings. She considered herself a poor shopper: "I have a fine genius for knowing that I have bought or ordered the wrong thing as soon as it is brought home." Their inconvenience hardly mattered. The place, Lewes wrote his "dear Johnnie," "is more ravishing than we fancied it—especially in this splendid weather—and the walks and drives are so much better than Society! (with a big S)." Blackwood, visiting them, found the view "perhaps finer than that from Richmond Hill" and Marian "looking well and full of happiness in the lovely spot where they are settled." He hoped, as he told her, that something should be born here and was pleased that she seemed to assent.

"Imagine me playing at lawn tennis by the hour together!" Marian exclaimed to Sara Hennell after returning to London in late autumn. She felt stronger than she had in years. Part of this improvement was attributed to Johnnie Cross, who had installed what Lewes called "an apparatus for Lawn-Tennis" at the Heights and taught them to play, insisting that they practice daily. He taught them badminton as well.

Writing to Marian's devoted fan Elma Stuart—now a close friend—Lewes pronounced their country place "a small paradise." He appended family news:

> *Charles and Gertrude have got another daughter—we wanted a grandson, but the superior powers thought otherwise.... The other day at dinner Madonna was talking with Bright* [unidentified] *about woman's suffrage, and the Princess Louise interposed with, "But you don't go in for the superiority of women, Mrs. Lewes?" "No."—"I think" said Huxley, "Mrs. Lewes rather teaches the inferiority of men."*

Soon the Leweses were saddened by the news that Mrs. Cross was dying. Marian consoled Johnnie gracefully: "The world cannot seem quite the same to me, as long as you are all in anxiety about her who is most precious to you.... For love is never without its shadow of anxiety."

Marian never had such high earning power. As the new year of 1878 dawned, Blackwood's sent Lewes (who did their banking) a check for more than £1,000 for sales of all George Eliot's novels during the past year. The Leweses were in the avantgarde not only of science but of the technological revolution. Having witnessed the arrival of the railway, the telegraph, and the photograph, they now saw two new advances. On March 21,

1878, Lewes escorted Marian to the Bell Telephone Company office in London and together they tried the telephone for an hour. "What marvellous inventions you Americans have!" she said politely. She was less admiring of the phonograph, Thomas Edison's invention of 1877, "which can report gentlemen's bad speeches with all their stammerings."

It was an exciting time to be alive, though Lewes continued to battle ill health. "My only real trouble," Marian told Elma in June 1878, is "that my Little Man is sadly out of health, racked with cramps from suppressed gout and feeling his inward economy all wrong." Lewes, now sixty-one, was suffering from cramps, piles, and bowel irritation. Sir James Paget, called in once more, knew it was bowel cancer; yet, true to the manners of a society physician, he did not utter the taboo word but declared the problem to be the "thickening of the mucous membrane." Cancer was unmentionable and carried a terrible stigma.

Lewes was now constantly ailing, seized at times with severe cramps. Yet bursts of pain did not prevent him from singing the tenor part of *The Barber of Seville* with Marian at the piano one evening at the Heights, nor from going over to the Tennysons' for lunch. Henry James, ever ready to pass on a cruel remark, heard from a visitor to Witley that Lewes looked as if he had been gnawed by rats.

For Marian, the summer and autumn at Witley had been spent writing eighteen essays and character sketches that would comprise her next book, an audacious collection of outspoken views on human nature and social attitudes, to be called *The Impressions of Theophrastus Such*. Borrowing the name of the

Greek philosopher who wrote acute sketches of various human types and appending the surname Such, Marian disguised herself as the unloved bachelor son of a Tory Midlands parson. Her Theophrastus reflects on the world around him and on various types of characters, attacking anti-Semitism and defending Jewish nationalism.

In early November, while their servants got the Priory in order, the Leweses managed a trip to Brighton to see Marian's niece Emily. When they returned, Lewes reported to John Blackwood that Mrs. Lewes was "pretty well, but has been horribly anxious about me."

She summoned Johnnie Cross, who left his mother's deathbed to come to the Lewes's to discuss Marian's investments. She turned over his remaining supply of cigars to be given to Cross's brother, Willie, a great smoker. Ever active as Marian's agent, Lewes asked her to show him the specimen pages of *Theophrastus*. He hooked a walking stick to the foot of his bed so that he could raise himself upright to read. Marian moved to a separate room so that he could have the bed to himself.

On November 21, Paget came before breakfast and left Lewes feeling better. As Lewes told his diary, "The storm has passed, I think!" So well did Lewes feel that he went out with their driver and posted off to Blackwood a portion of the manuscript of *Theophrastus*, the kind of errand that Marian did not do for herself. But the exertion tired him; he caught a chill and ended up back in bed. He still hoped that his illness—"a fluctuating sickness with much malaise and headache"—was transitory.

On November 29, Paget brought along another fashionable doctor and together they pronounced Lewes "in every respect better." But by night, he was worse again. On November 30, just before six in the evening, the man who gave the world George Eliot was dead. He died unaware of what Paget had already told his son: cancer would have killed him within six months. The irony is glaring. The rigid conventions of the time that had prevented George Henry Lewes from marrying the woman he loved had also kept him ignorant to the last of the disease that ended his life.

For Marian's sake, perhaps the pretense was just as well. Devastated by her loss, she could not face the funeral at the chapel in Highgate Cemetery. There, Lewes, as a rationalist, was laid to rest in unconsecrated ground, where he would soon be joined by his Polly and, not long after, by Karl Marx.

## Chapter Thirteen

# NEAR-DEATH IN VENICE (1879–1880)

L ETTERS OF CONDOLENCE poured in. Browning, Tennyson, and the Viceroy of India (Robert, Lord Lytton) were among the many who sent sympathy, few as sweepingly as the Russian novelist Ivan Turgenev. A frequent visitor to the Priory, Turgenev assured Marian, "All your friends, all learned Europe mourn with you." Herbert Spencer, as if reminding Marian that he had spurned the chance to become her husband, confessed that he could only "dimly conceive what such a parting must be" especially "in a case where two lives have been so long bound together so closely, in such multitudinous ways." Her women friends rallied round—Mrs. Thomas Trollope, Bessie Parkes (now Madame Louis Belloc) and Barbara Bodichon, to whom in letters of reply she described herself as "Your loving but half dead Marian." There was even a letter from Nuneaton; her sister-in-law, Sarah Evans, wife of Marian's unforgiving brother Isaac, wrote from Griff House expressing her heartache "in your sad bereavement."

For a time Marian could not face reading any of the letters. Severely depressed, she also had an attack of kidney pain and for three months hardly left her room. She ate very little; her weight dropped to just above a hundred pounds. The Priory's cook gossiped to the neighbors about howls that could be heard throughout the house.

It was more than grief that overwhelmed her. Her George had been her galvanizer, her secretary, her bookkeeper. She had rarely gone out the door without him beside her. Like royalty, she never carried money; he had handled all the intricacies of subsidizing his extended family and hers. His son Charlie, who had grown ever closer to his stepmother, tried to take this burden from her.

One man who was permitted to call was Sir James Paget. "Talked of my darling," she noted of the doctor's visit. "Dreadfully depressed. Unable to do anything all evening." Although Paget, still avoiding the ugly word, had certified the cause of death as "enteritis" (inflammation of the small intestine), a postmortem had revealed the cancer, and Marian was now told. She was relieved that her George had at least been spared the ordeal of prolonged pain and the knowledge that he was dying. Apart from Paget, she saw no one but Charles.

Nearly two months passed before she felt able to write three brief sentences to the person best able to help her, Johnnie Cross. "Dearest Nephew," she wrote toward the end of January 1879. "Some time, if I live, I shall be able to see you—perhaps sooner than any one else—but not yet. Life seems to get harder instead of easier." The two shared a bond of grief. Cross's mother, to whom he had been devoted, had died nine days after Lewes.

At last, on February 22, Marian wrote that she would see Cross sometime within the following week. He came the next day, a Sunday. Spencer, calling at the Priory the same day, was turned away with the message that Mrs. Lewes was not ready to receive friends.

There was much for Cross to deal with, principally Lewes's financial affairs. The *Times* on January 3, 1879, carried, under "Wills and Bequests," the news that the will "of Mr. George Henry Lewes, the celebrated author, formerly of Holly-lodge South Fields, Wandsworth but late of the Priory, North Bank, Regent's Park, who died on November 30 last, was proved on the 16th ult. by Miss Mary Ann Evans, the sole executrix." The newspaper tactfully omitted the will's description of Marian as "Spinster."

This open publication of their most shameful secret mortified Marian's Warwickshire family. The revelation that she still bore her maiden name also startled those of their friends who had assumed that "the Leweses" had somehow married on the Continent.

It is odd that Lewes, with his shrewd business sense, had not appreciated that, as Marian was not his legal wife, she would have no access to her own money. Both their homes—in London and in Witley—were in his name alone, as were all her earnings, along with securities worth more than £30,000.

To prove the will and to take control of her own funds, Marian had to change her name by deed poll to Mary Ann Evans Lewes.

Once Marian had her hands on the funds, she swiftly allotted £5,000 to establish the George Henry Lewes Studentship in Physiology at Cambridge University to assist gifted students in the field he had loved. The grant was to be available to women as well as men in consideration of the opening of Cambridge's first women's college, Girton. (However, a grant was not awarded to a woman until forty years later.) These transactions invigorated her. She moved back to the bedroom she had shared with Lewes, put his books in order, and packed away his microscope.

Marian got back to work. She corrected the proofs of her new book of essays, *Impressions of Theophrastus Such*, and tidied up the rough manuscript of the third volume of Lewes's magnum opus, *Problems of Life and Mind*, which presented the mind as a property of the nervous system. She worked exhaustively, fearful that she would not complete it to his standard. Gently, John Blackwood reminded her that Lewes had wanted her book published as well as his own.

Her admirer Edith Simcox became obsessed with the thought of her beloved sequestered in sorrow in the Priory. She called at the gates almost daily, her eyes full of tears, and grilled the maid and the housekeeper for any scrap of information about Mrs. Lewes. At last, on April 12, 1879, she was admitted with more warmth than before and was bidden to sit on a footstool, whereupon, as Edith gratefully told her diary, "she took my hand in hers." Marian's devotee from France, Elma Stuart, also came to pay her respects.

Marian paid several visits to Lewes's grave at Highgate Cemetery and arranged to have ivy and jasmine planted around the stone. At times she fell into a mental conversation with him so vivid that she almost believed she saw his ghost.

Having lost the love of her life, the last thing Marian needed was more dependents. However, in April, Bertie Lewes's widow, Eliza, arrived from Natal with her small children—Marian and George. They stayed with Charlie in Hampstead. Eliza seemed to think, perhaps because she had named her children after their famous grandparents, that she might be invited to live at the Priory.

Marian had the family to lunch and took them home to Hampstead in her carriage, but discouraged hints that they share her home. She found "the little Africans," as she referred to them, beautiful but wild. When Eliza began complaining about England, Marian heartily wished that she would go back to Natal, though to no avail. Despite the monthly checks she sent, relations remained uneasy.

Eliza's arrival had added to Marian's feelings of oppression and prevented her from returning to her country house. Determined, as she wrote Barbara Bodichon, "to live as bravely as I can," every day she had herself driven in her carriage to the (then) green spaces of London beyond Kilburn "where I can walk in perfect privacy among the fields and budding hedgerows."

She had by now a great number to support, including her sister Chrissey's daughter Emily, Lewes's nephew Edward, and, as ever, Agnes Lewes, Lewes's legal widow, who received a quarterly payment of £100. There was enough money for all, but not enough time and space.

Marian summoned Johnnie Cross urgently; never was her need for a man to lean on so undisguised. "Dearest N.: I am in dreadful need of your counsel. Pray come to me when you can—morning, afternoon, or evening. I shall dismiss anyone else." She signed herself "Your much worried Aunt." Then, nervously, she fretted. Had her letter gone to the right place? Was Johnnie at his club (the City Liberal Club) or in Weybridge, or away on a visit?

From that time on, she and Cross saw each other constantly. Seeking a new interest (and perhaps a new mother), he told Marian that, although he hardly knew any Italian, he was taking up the study of Dante. "Oh, I must read that with you," she replied. So they began. Line by line, she leading and he following, they got from the *Inferno* through to the *Purgatorio*. In the months that followed, Cross felt, as he later wrote, "the divine poet took us into a new world."

Marian's diary for May 16, 1879, shows a single word: "Crisis." This terse entry has stirred strong and enduring speculation that she had discovered that Lewes had been unfaithful to her. Rumors had, in fact, started long before, owing to Lewes's constant dining out unaccompanied and his obvious pleasure in the company of pretty women. There has been no evidence to support this theory, however. There is, instead, ample evidence that Marian's crisis was a medical one; her entry for the following two days reads "Severe attack of pain." When Edith Simcox visited on Sunday, May 18, she found her beloved Mrs. Lewes "with a deathlike expression of overpast [*sic*] pain."

Marian left the Priory for Witley on May 22, steeled for the sadness of returning to the rural surroundings where she and her George had been so happy. Johnnie Cross was ever on hand to speed her recovery, and at his urging, on May 27, she played the piano again for the first time since Lewes's death. To her dear friend Georgiana Burne-Jones, she wrote that Cross was "a devoted friend who is backwards and forwards continually to see that I lack nothing." Yet against all rational inclination, she found herself again overwhelmed by Lewes's closeness. "His presence came again," she noted in her diary on May 28.

By happy coincidence, copies of each of their new books—Lewes's *Problems of Life and Mind* and her own *Impressions of Theophrastus Such*—had reached her before she left London. It was already arranged that *Theophrastus Such* would be translated into Dutch and German, and Marian was well enough to involve herself in these editions. She pointed out to William Blackwood that her books were being read more widely throughout Germany, urging him not to ask too low a price.

Without Lewes to read reviews for her, Marian may not have seen the superb one for *Theophrastus Such* in the *Times* on June 5, 1879. But the Blackwoods read it with delight. On June 11, 1879, in a long essay marveling at the book, the *Times* described it as "emphatically a work of genius—the fruit of deep thought and ripe experience, of research, observation, and ingenious speculation." The subject, the reviewer said, was grave, but there was a bright sparkle in its style. He was particularly moved by the last and most eloquent sketch, devoted to the barbaric and humiliating persecution of the Jews in the Dark Ages, treatment that failed to extinguish "a feeling of race and a sense of corporate existence unique in their intensity." As it turned out, Marian's essay titled "The Modern Hep! Hep! Hep!," echoing the Crusaders' cry for conquering Jerusalem, was the only one of the collection to be translated into German, with the subtitle *"Juden und ihre Gegnern."* It was widely circulated.

In July, Marian suffered another bout of ill health. After her symptoms had persisted for four weeks, Sir James Paget went to Witley to visit her, as did her other London doctor, Andrew Clark. She was ordered to try to put on weight and to drink a pint of champagne a day, a prescription she found preferable to "the poisonous concoctions" she had previously been given as medicine.

Writing letters from bed, she was strong enough to try to dissuade her "Dearest Boy" Charlie Lewes and his family from going to Wales for their holiday: "I cannot bear to think of your being fixed for your one good holiday in rainy Wales, where the Methodists sing out of tune and there is a general aspect of moral dreariness." She reported that she was now stronger in body, but more depressed in mind.

There was some consolation in learning from Blackwood's that more than eighteen thousand copies of all her books, including *Theophrastus Such*, had been sold in the six months from January to June 1879.

People kept writing to George Eliot asking for photographs. Refusing one request, she said (concealing the truth) that her reason was "not that I am ashamed of the physiognomy which nature has given me," but rather a fear of being recognized and stared at in public. She also asked Charlie to answer "an unconsciously impertinent American" autograph-hunter with an official letter saying that "Mrs. Lewes (George Eliot), whom he has mistakenly addressed as Miss Marian Evans, has no photograph of herself and systematically abstains from giving her autograph."

Marian continued to console herself with Johnnie Cross's company. Between their common interests in Dante and the piano, he felt himself falling in love with her. Or, as he wrote in his biography of Marian, "It was a renovation of life." Her feelings rushed to match. "Decisive conversation," she wrote in her diary on August 21, 1879. By October, she was able to write to Elma Stuart, "My health is wonderfully better." She felt stronger than she had for a year and a half.

Also in October, Marian wrote Cross a love letter. Excruciating to read, with its half-English, half-German baby talk, its wording recalls the unguarded declaration of love she had sent Herbert Spencer nearly thirty years before. "Best loved and loving one— the sun it shines so cold, so cold, when there are no eyes to look love on me. I cannot bear to sadden one moment when we are together, but wenn Du bist nicht da [when you are not here] I have often a bad time."

Marian acknowledged, however, their age difference— she was nearly sixty, he not yet forty. She wrote to him that a short while ago he was just "in pantaloons and back hair." She accepted that he was not learned in philosophy or science, "but thou knowest best things of another sort, such as belong to the manly heart—secrets of lovingness and rectitude." In her letters to him, she signed herself "thy tender Beatrice" to his Dante. With less than a year having passed since Lewes's death, these passionate letters were written incongruously on black-bordered mourning paper.

Lovingness and rectitude did not prevent another bout of illness. Yet despite chill and headache, she found reasons to be cheerful. She enjoyed the fact that Cross was playing tennis, a sign of his vigor, and was also happy to hear that the Cambridge trustees had chosen an Edinburgh physiologist for the first Lewes Studentship.

Sad news soon arrived from Edinburgh, however. John Blackwood, the man who, next to Lewes, had been her staunchest supporter, had died on October 29, 1879, of a heart attack, at the age of sixty-one. He had had the satisfaction of seeing *Theophrastus Such* swiftly run into three editions before he died.

It was a heavy loss. Marian told Charlie, "He has been bound up with what I most cared for in my life for more than twenty years and his good qualities have made many things easy for me that might have been difficult."

Back in London in November, Marian saw Cross frequently. In her solitary afternoons she went to Hampstead to see Bertie's widow and children. At home, she received Maria Congreve, her former neighbor from Wandsworth, who had turned into another worshipper and who now found herself overcome with trembling whenever she saw her beloved.

Marian passed her sixtieth birthday alone. A week later, on the first anniversary of Lewes's death, she spent the day in the room where she had closeted herself for the first three months of mourning. She read his old letters and packed them to be buried with her. "Perhaps that will happen before next November," she forecast. She was not far wrong.

Writing to her old Coventry friend, Sara Hennell, she declared that while she was blessed in many ways, even more blessed were the dead "who have not to dread a barren useless survival." Was this an admission of a writer who knew she would write no more? *Theophrastus Such* was to be her last book.

With her life drawing to a close, she once more expressed her revulsion for the entire genre of biography in a letter to Mrs. Thomas Trollope:

> *The best history of a writer is contained in his writings—these are his chief actions. If he happens to have left an autobiography telling (what nobody else can tell) how his mind grew, how it was determined by the joys, sorrows and other influences of childhood and youth—that is a precious contribution to knowledge. But Biographies generally are a disease of English literature.*

Did she anticipate that more than a century later biographers would be retracing the growth of her love for Cross and her hesitating steps to the altar?

During Christmas 1879, she stayed alone at the Priory, "smelling the servants' goose." Asking Cross to dine with her when he returned to town, she wrote, "Will you do me that honour?" and signed herself "Your obliged ex-shareholder of A and C Gaslight and Coke." Cross had just sold her shares worth £1,200 in this company, and there was more money on the way. In February 1880, William Blackwood sent Marian a bank order for £784 10 shillings 8 pence (about $85,000 today) for royalties due her.[1]

By now, Cross was Marian's steady companion. Together they went to the National Gallery and the South Kensington museums, enjoying the bond of mutual dependence that had formed between them. Edith Simcox noticed a change in her attitude when she called on March 9 and went through her usual routine. "I ventured to kneel by her side...kissed her again and again and murmured broken words of love," whereupon Marian rebuffed her, explaining for the first time that "she had never all her life cared very much for women...the friendship and intimacy of men was more to her."

Marian's diary explains the change in her outlook. She noted on April 9, 1880, that Paget had come to see her, whereupon she appears to have sought medical reassurance on the advisability of a sixty-year-old marrying a man who had just turned forty. Paget's response must have been positive. "My marriage decided," she wrote afterward.

Though conscious of the age difference in her situation, Marian herself had long supported such alliances for others. Nearly three years earlier, in a letter to Barbara Bodichon, Marian had applauded the marriage of Thackeray's daughter Anne to a man nearly twenty years her junior. Dismissing the age gap as "bridged hopefully by his solidarity and gravity," she told of several similar matches "showing that young men with even brilliant advantages will often choose as their life's companion a woman whose attractions are wholly of the spiritual order." The remark shows that Marian did not expect such May-December marriages to be sexual. It also begs the question: Had she spotted "nephew Johnnie" as a replacement husband even before Lewes's death? Her Positivist friends the Harrisons told others they suspected that she had got tired of Lewes and had turned to Cross before Lewes died.[2]

What delighted Marian most about her new status as a fiancée was the prospect of becoming not only a wife but a member of a family. All the Cross family welcomed the news of Johnnie's engagement to the famous author. To her prospective sister-in-law Eleanor Cross, Marian wrote, "You can hardly think how sweet the name Sister is to me, that I have not been called by for so many, many years." After a quarter of a century, her brother's rejection still stung. She saw this new chance at a family as a "wonderful renewal of my life. Nothing less than the prospect of being loved and welcomed by you could have sustained me. But now I cherish the thought that the family life will be the richer and not the poorer through your Brother's great gift of love to me."

Her efforts at self-beautification were noticed and mocked. Marian shopped for a trousseau so energetically that Tennyson's daughter-in-law coldly observed that "whatever money and taste could do to make her look not too unsuitable a bride for a man of forty had been done." Her habit of covering her massive head with a delicate lace mantilla or a flouncy hat produced a contrast that, the writer Edmund Gosse commented, was "pathetic and provincial."

The affianced couple wasted no time. The day after they decided to marry, they went to look at a house in Chelsea and within weeks had bought it: a gracious five-story redbrick Georgian house overlooking the Thames at 4 Cheyne Walk.[3]

The day before her marriage, Marian wrote to William Blackwood and her close female friends about the change in her life. Georgiana Burne-Jones was hurt at not having been told of the wedding until the very last minute. Barbara Bodichon and Bessie Parkes Belloc were more sympathetic and congratulated her. Barbara wrote charitably that she knew that Mr. Lewes would be glad of the marriage; that, moreover, if she were a man, she would have done just what John Cross had done. They did not find her choice of a handsome young bachelor any more discordant than her choice of Lewes, the bewhiskered little rake, a quarter of a century earlier. In those pre-Freudian days, no one suggested overattachment to his mother as a possible explanation for Cross's prolonged bachelorhood. He was eminently respectable, a banker with a public school education.

At quarter past ten in the morning on Thursday, May 6, 1880, on the arm of her "Dearest Boy," Charlie Lewes, Marian walked down the aisle of St. George's, Hanover Square. Agnosticism gave way to the convention of an Anglican service and Marian, at the age of sixty, became a married woman at last. Charlie was entirely sympathetic to the marriage. He told his friends that he owed everything to this woman. Many members of the Cross family were at the church: Cross's brother William and his two brothers-in-law signed the register as witnesses. The bride and groom were described respectively as "Spinster" and "Bachelor"; his profession was given as "Merchant"; hers was left blank. His father was listed as "Merchant," hers as "Surveyor."

Afterward, the newlyweds went back to the Priory, signed their wills, and left to spend a few months abroad. They caught the train to Dover and were there by five o'clock. The next morning they took a deck cabin for what turned out to be a calm crossing to Calais. Marian wrote to Charlie that marriage had seemed to restore her old self.

Charlie was deputized to break the news of the marriage to Marian's trio of devotees—Edith Simcox, Maria Congreve, and Elma Stuart—knowing that they would not welcome it. The Congreves were very shocked, Maria particularly, as Positivist belief held that the dead lived on in the minds of the living. In their view, by taking a new husband so soon, Marian was betraying the memory of Lewes. And while they acknowledged that she had given Positivism only intellectual support, they were surprised that she chose a Church of England ceremony. Cross, meanwhile, wrote to Elma saying that he could think of nothing "except how marvelously blessed is my lot—to be united for life with her who has for so long been my ideal."

One person who was true to his religion was Marian's brother, Isaac. Now that his sister had been married with benefit of clergy, he allowed himself to write to her for the first time in thirty-three years. In a letter that reached her in Milan on her honeymoon, he expressed much pleasure in "the present opportunity to break the long silence which has existed between us" and wished her "happiness and comfort." In closing, he wrote, "Believe me Your affectionate brother Isaac P. Evans."

The letter filled her with joy. She thanked him for his kind words of sympathy,

*for our long silence has never broken the affection for you which began when we were little ones. My Husband too was much pleased to read your letter. I have known his family for nine years, and they have received me amongst them very lovingly. He is of a most solid, well tried character and has had a great deal of experience. The only point to be regretted in our marriage is that I am much older than he but his affection has made him choose this lot of caring for me rather than any other of the various lots open to him.*

Marian and Johnnie's honeymoon was "a chapter of delights—Grenoble—Grande Chartreuse—Chambéry—paradisial walk to Les Charmettes—etc.," Marian wrote from Italy to her new sister-in-law, Florence Cross. Much as she and Lewes had done during their first trip abroad, she and Cross assiduously toured museums and churches; this time, however, she took the lead, introducing her new husband to delights he had not seen before.

Whether she was able to introduce him to the delights of the marriage bed, however, is not known. The many letters they wrote during the honeymoon nonetheless paint an idyllic picture. Aping his predecessor, Cross referred to his wife as "mia Donna." From Verona, he informed his sister Mary, "we have not talked to another soul since we left England." He was looking forward to their time in Venice: "I don't know what people generally complain so much of in their wedding journeys—ours has certainly been very full of delight and it goes on increasing and I hope will go on *jusqu'à la fin*—she is a very inexhaustible storehouse."

On the June 4, 1880, the *Gazzetta di Venezia*, which carried news of visitors to Venice, listed a couple named Cross among the seven English families who had checked into the Hotel Europa that day.[4] A late Gothic palace, it was built at the end of the fifteenth century and transformed into the Hotel Europa in 1830. The Europa drew many famous guests, including Giuseppe Verdi, Marcel Proust, and Théophile Gautier. In 1858 the composer Richard Wagner stayed there while writing the second act of *Tristan and Isolde*. Once settled in, the Crosses hired their own gondola and gondolier and for twelve days looked at pictures and churches and cruised about the waterways. Their cheerful letters home, however, did not tell the whole story. Cross was not responding well to the city. He had lost much weight prior to the wedding and Marian could see that he was now in poor condition, alternately agitated and deeply depressed. On the morning of June 16, Marian, alarmed by his demeanor, summoned a doctor and recited her husband's symptoms.

She even suggested (probably from personal knowledge) to the Italian physician, Dr. Ricchetti, that there might be insanity in the Cross family. Certainly Cross's subsequent actions seem to support this suspicion. While she and the doctor were talking in an interior room, Cross went out onto the balcony of their hotel suite, clambered up on the railing and hurled himself into the Grand Canal. It was half past eleven in the morning.

Cross leaped with such force that he sailed over the three or four gondolas stationed outside the hotel and landed in the middle of the canal. Corradini, their gondolier, immediately threw himself into the water, as did one of the Europa hotel staff. Together the men rescued him and carried him back to his rooms.

The incident made at least two Venetian newspapers, which reported that "an Englishman of about forty years of age," suffering from a permanent melancholy, had at half past eleven in the morning "thrown himself from the first floor of the Hotel Europa" and was saved by a gondolier named Corradini.

The afternoon paper, *Il Tempo*, invited its readers to imagine "the desolation of the poor wife!" with no hint that the "poor wife" ("*povera sposa*") was the most famous English novelist of the day. The Englishman had suffered no contusions, *Il Tempo* continued, and had recovered full exercise of his faculties. The next day, another paper, *L'Adriatico*, described the incident and attributed the apparent suicide attempt to "*una mania malinconica.*" "One could say that he had a lucky escape!" it concluded.

The San Marco police station classified the incident as a suicide attempt. The inspector for the commissariat of San Marco was struck by the age difference between husband and wife and noted it in his report. Translated, it reads:

> J. W. Cross, an Englishman of 40 years, had been lodged for two weeks at the Hotel Europa with his wife, a woman over sixty. For some days he had been looking sad and melancholy, prompting his wife to call in a doctor. While they were talking, the husband, in the next room, made the aforementioned attempt on his life.

The *inglese*, the police report continued, was found to be lavishly supplied with money, as well as with cards giving him unlimited credit at major banks. It appeared that three years previously he had suffered a similar attack—*una peripezia* or sudden change in personality. The inspector concluded his report by stating that the aforementioned individual had regained his normal health.

Shattered, Marian sent two telegrams to her brother-in-law, William Cross, summoning him to Venice. Willie arrived on June 18. The doctor prescribed chloral, a powerful sedative popular at the time, for Cross, and the honeymoon continued, with William in tow, all three of them blaming the heat and odorous canals of Venice for the dramatic incident.

In London, where it was merely rumored that Cross was ill, Edith Simcox would later pry more information from the Cross sisters, whom she went down to Weybridge to interview, having heard that Cross had typhoid. Johnnie was apparently very weak: "they carried him by slow stages out of Venice. Munich did not suit him, but he was out of danger now, had written one letter himself, they were going to Wildbad and likely to be back as proposed the end of the month."

No suggestion of suicide appeared in any of Marian's letters to her friends, or in Cross's biography of his late wife, published in 1885:

> We thought too little of the heat, and rather laughed at English people's dread of the sun. It is one thing to enjoy heat when leading an active life...another to spend all one's days in a gondola...and with bedroom-windows always open on the great drain of the Grand Canal....The effect of this continual bad air, and the complete and sudden deprivation of all bodily exercise, made me thoroughly ill. As soon as I could move we left Venice, on the 23rd of June, and went to Innsbruck....[In the] pure sweet mountain air, I soon regained strength.

Marian wrote to Elma Stuart from Innsbruck on June 27, 1880, that "Mr. Cross had an attack of illness, due chiefly to the influences of the climate and to the lack of muscular exercise which the allurements of the gondola bring with them." Any whiff of attempted suicide would inevitably have raised the question of Marian's vanity in imagining that she could be a satisfying wife for a much younger man. Yet her wry and very English blame on the "allurements of the gondola" reveals her skill in rendering the dark side of life in graceful and well-chosen words.

Although news of the incident did not reach the English papers, it nevertheless leaked out in gossip. Speculation was irresistible. As recounted in the memoirs of Walter Sichel, political biographer and attorney, "after a prolonged course of Dante at Venice he [Cross] had cast himself into the Grand Canal and begged the gondoliers not to rescue him."

A lively fictionalized account of the scene that many must have imagined appeared in *Johnnie Cross*, a 1983 novel by Terence de Vere White. Subtitled *The Intriguing Story behind George Eliot's Mysterious Last Year*, it depicts the haggard, aged wife aggressively demanding her marital rights from an inexperienced bachelor. The young husband glimpses his bride drawing back her robe and staring at her naked self in a mirror:

> The large face above made the white, shrivelled body look as if it belonged to somebody else—pathetic in its thinness, vulnerable in its nakedness; what little flesh there was clung loosely to the large-boned frame, from which the breasts like dry wrinkled figs hung low; there were deep creases across the flaccid stomach. I took it all in as I turned my eyes away and stepped back, but not quickly enough to escape a glimpse of a sad grey mat and thighs as thin as arms.

A more trustworthy note on the incident survives in the papers of Lord Acton. A historian and writer, Acton knew the Cross family through the Tennysons and became a personal friend of John Cross, who, indeed, may himself have given Acton an account of the event. In undated notes left at the University Library at Cambridge, where he later became Regius Professor of Modern History, Acton wrote, "At Venice she thought him mad, and she never recovered [from] the dreadful depression that followed. Sent for Ricchetti, told him that Cross had a mad brother. Told her fears. Just then, heard that he had jumped into the Canal."

All told, it seems unlikely that the marriage of Mr. and Mrs. John Cross was ever consummated. Yet regarding Cross's admiration, even adoration, of the great writer he had married, there is no doubt. Like Henry James, he seems to have found himself "literally in love with this great horse-faced blue-stocking," but it was love without desire.

## Chapter Fourteen

# KEEPER OF THE FLAME (1880–1884)

THE CROSSES RETURNED from their honeymoon on July 26, 1880, to their Surrey home, where they received friends and relatives just like any newly married couple. They visited Cross's sisters in Kent, Lincolnshire, and Cambridgeshire. At a dinner party given for them in Cambridge, Caroline Jebb, the wife of the eminent classicist Richard Claverhouse Jebb, observed the famous pair closely and sent her sister a catty but perceptive report:

> *George Eliot, old as she is, and ugly, really looked very sweet and winning in spite of both. She was dressed in a short soft satin walking dress with a lace wrap half shading the body, a costume most artistically designed to show her slenderness, yet hiding the squareness of age.*

As the evening wore on, Mrs. Jebb began to feel sorry for the guest of honor.

> *There was not a person in the room, Mr. Cross included, whose mother she might not have been. . . . She adores her husband, and it*

*seemed to me it hurt her a little to have him talk so much to me. It made her, in her pain, slightly irritated and snappish. . . . He may forget the twenty years difference between them, but she never can.*

Mrs. Jebb judged that the marriage was "against nature" and concluded, "She has cultivated every art to make herself attractive, feeling bitterly all the time what a struggle it was, without beauty, whose influence she exaggerates as do all ugly people." On the other hand, she liked Mr. Cross very much: "He is tall, fine looking, a good talker, altogether an exceptionally interesting man."

Marriage had done little to improve Marian's health. In October, Cross took her to Brighton for ten days with little benefit. Back at Witley, Marian felt such pain that she took "an opiate." She was so unwell that her London doctor, Andrew Clark, came down to see her.

Her new husband's attention was, however, compensation for her suffering. To Charlie Lewes, she wrote that she felt "cared for in every way with miraculous tenderness." With no sense of imputing effeminacy, and proud of his uxoriousness, she informed her friend Barbara Bodichon that Mr. Cross had nursed her "as if he had been a wife nursing a husband." She boasted, too, about his exuberant health: at the Heights he was laying out a tennis court, where he played daily. To Cara Bray she announced that "Mr. Cross . . . is exceedingly well and strong now, and cuts down a thickish tree in half an hour."

There was more to Marian's boasting than mere pride, however. She was determined that Cross exercise to fend off a recurrence of the Venetian melancholia, and also to keep his weight down. On the days when lawn tennis was impossible, she told Charles that she and Johnnie, as she allowed herself to call him in family letters, played indoor battledore and shuttlecock in their high drawing room. Even so, there was still a line in his cheek which, she told his sister Anna, "I long to see raised to smoothness."

Cross went up to London almost every day, as there was much to organize in shifting books, china, and pictures out of the Priory and into their new house on Cheyne Walk, where they planned to spend the winter. Worrying like a nervous mother every minute when he was out of her sight, Marian met his train with a carriage and driver in the afternoon when he returned.

Packing up at Witley, she congratulated Cara, who had written of burning old letters. Marian said she hoped that she herself had removed as many as possible from the prying eyes of posterity. (How many she can have destroyed is a good question, for enough survived to fill nine published volumes of *Letters of George Eliot*.)

If she was depressed, however, Marian concealed it well in her letters. As her sixty-first birthday approached, she wrote Cara how grateful she was that her life should have been prolonged enough to allow her the joy of being surrounded by family love and especially to enjoy the "dual companionship" at her own hearth. On her birthday, reading aloud together, the dual companions finished Herbert Spencer's *Study of Sociology* and began Max Müller's *Lectures on the Science of Language*, which she herself had read several years before.

At the end of November, Cross decided that they must move up to London to supervise the furnishing of the new house and to engage servants. As their house was not quite ready, they checked into Bailey's Hotel in South Kensington. Marian, still full of the joys of family, thanked her "Dear Brother" Willie Cross for warning them that the resident housekeeper at Cheyne Walk was addicted to gin. She signed herself (adopting yet another new name) "Your affectionate Sister M. A. Cross."

By December 3, they were installed at last in their Georgian home, where they enjoyed "the outlook on the river and meadows beyond" and the warmth, compared with Witley. After their first dinner under their new roof, the Crosses continued their joint reading—a translation of *Don Quixote* was their choice— and the next day, a Saturday, they attended a Pop Concert at St. James's Hall. To Sara Hennell, Marian vented her opinion that Mozart was inclined to "the Italian 'sugared view' in contrast with Handel, Beethoven and Schubert."

Four days later, however, Marian was alarmed when Cross was laid up with a cold and a fever along with an affliction with which she was all too familiar—"a bilious attack." As he recovered, she began inviting friends to call on them in their new home and made their plans for Christmas: they would spend it with some of Cross's family at Sevenoaks, Kent.

On December 18, husband and wife went to see a performance of *Agamemnon* (in Greek, by Oxford undergraduates) and the next day they attended another Pop Concert. Four days later, Marian was dead.

For someone so often ill, death arrived without warning. On Sunday, December 19, in spite of a slight sore throat, Marian had been visited, at her invitation, by Herbert Spencer and Edith Simcox. Edith had not seen her since before her marriage and on their reunion wrote, "I was too shy to ask for any special greeting—only kissed her again and again as she sat. Mr. Cross came in soon and I noticed his countenance was transfigured, a calm look of pure beatitude had succeeded the ordinary good nature."

The next day, a general practitioner, sent by Andrew Clark because he lived nearby, noted that she had a severe sore throat and difficulty swallowing. The following day he found her better, however, and diagnosed an "ordinary 3 days laryngitical sore throat." That night she had a disturbed sleep with pain in her right kidney. Wednesday found her weak and drowsy, but she was bolstered by some jellied beef consommé and an egg beaten up with brandy. Later that day, Dr. Clark called. Where his colleague had seen little to concern him, Clark did not hesitate in his diagnosis. There was little hope, he told Cross. Inflammation had arisen in the heart and the surrounding fluid sac, the pericardium. At that point Marian woke and said, "Tell them I have great pain in the left side."

Those were her last words. Soon afterward she lapsed into unconsciousness. Just before ten o'clock that night she died.

CROSS sprang immediately to his duties as a widower. Before midnight on the day of her death, December 22, 1880, he wrote to Isaac Evans, the brother-in-law he had never met, to tell him "that your noble sister and my wife died this night a little before 10 o'clock." He added, generously and truly, "one of the most gratifying collateral incidents of our marriage was that it broke the long silence that had existed between you and your sister." Cross described himself as "quite dazed" but insisted, "I feel that you should be written to first of all."

That same night he wrote to Georgiana Burne-Jones to tell her that her great friend and his dear wife had died "with a frightful suddenness" that had left him stunned. To Elma Stuart, with the directness and charming turn of phrase that would make him a worthy biographer, Cross said he wished to spare her the shock of seeing the announcement in the newspapers. He described the death scene and its last moments, then said, "And I am left alone in this new House we meant to be so happy in."

On Christmas Eve, Friday, December 24, the *Times* gave George Eliot a long, respectful obituary:

> A great English writer has suddenly passed away. "George Eliot," to give her the name by which Mrs. Cross was known wherever the English language is spoken or English literature is prized, died on Wednesday evening, after only three days' illness. On Sunday evening last she received the visits of several old friends at the house in Cheyne-walk which she and her husband (to whom she was only married last May) had lately occupied and when they left her she was apparently in good health and spirits.

The *Times* described the doctors' visits and diagnosis, then said that little was known of the details of the writer's life. It mentioned her books, her Warwickshire birth, her father, Robert Evans, land agent and surveyor who, it said, was still remembered "as a man of rare worth and character by many neighbors in the Midlands." She seemed to have come to London, it continued, "almost as a girl, and to have devoted herself to serious literature in a manner far more common among women of the present day than it was nearly 40 years ago." It mentioned her first serious work, the translation of Strauss's *Das Leben Jesu*, which exhibited an equal mastery of German and English. It listed the group of writers who were her fellow contributors to the *Westminster Review*—George Henry Lewes among them—and went on to say that Lewes had sent *Scenes of Clerical Life*—"her first imaginative work"—anonymously to *Blackwood's Edinburgh Magazine*.

The obituary also saw fit to comment on the late writer's physical appearance: her gracious manner and winning smile "irradiated features that were too strongly marked for feminine beauty." But, it concluded, "her memory lies in the gratitude of countless thousands of readers, and the thought of the life of a great and noble woman suddenly cut off in the promise of renewed happiness will sadden many a household in the midst of Christmas rejoicings."

The paper's leader page also carried a lengthy analysis of George Eliot's novels, making clear that *The Mill on the Floss* was its favorite. It retraced the Liggins controversy about the authorship of *Adam Bede* and discreetly mentioned that George Eliot was actually Marian Evans, known to her intimates as "Mrs. Lewes." It praised the "almost boundless range of her regard for humanity" and singled out her portraits of peasants and clergy for their tenderness without sentimentality.

Cross, in notifying Herbert Spencer of Marian's death, raised the possibility of a burial in Westminster Abbey. Spencer loyally sent a telegram to the Dean of the Abbey, but the suggestion got nowhere. The agnostic T. H. Huxley accurately pointed out that

George Eliot was not only a great writer but a person known for her "notorious antagonism to Christian practice in regard to marriage." As such, she could not expect burial in a Christian sacred place: "One cannot eat one's cake and have it too." The unconsecrated section of Highgate Cemetery was the obvious solution.[1]

A procession of coaches formed for the long drive across London from Cheyne Walk to Highgate where, in the cemetery's chapel, Lewes's service of two years earlier served as a model: "most of the order of the Prayer Book with discreet Unitarian omissions," as Marian's biographer Gordon Haight described it. After a reading of "O May I Join the Choir Invisible," Marian's body was buried near Lewes, her grave touching his at one corner. Lewes's letters were, as she had wished, buried with her.

There was a sizeable crowd of onlookers, in addition to notable mourners who included Robert Browning, Huxley, Sir Charles Dilke (Member of Parliament for Chelsea), Lord Arthur Russell, Spencer, and William Blackwood. Marian's assorted families were represented by Charlie Lewes, Isaac Evans and his clergyman son, and various Cross relatives. The inscription on the coffin lopped a year off her age as Marian had often done— showing her birth year as 1820, rather than 1819. The indomitable Edith Simcox managed a final kiss on the coffin.

On February 18, 1881, the *Times* reported "Mrs. Mary Ann Cross (George Eliot), wife of John Walter Cross, late of No. 4, Cheyne-walk, Chelsea" left a personal estate of £40,000 (about $4,400,000 today). Charles Lee Lewes was sole executor. Marian's strong sense of responsibility for her own family and for Lewes's never deserted her. She left nothing to Cross— presumably as agreed. He was a successful banker, well off in his own right, and was aware of the contents of the will signed on their wedding day. Instead, Marian's money was divided among those who needed it. The largest sum, £12,000, went to Eliza Lewes, Bertie's widow from Natal, who had two small children to raise. Another £3,000 went to Marian's own niece, Emily Clarke; £1,000 to Lewes's nephew (his brother Edward's son, Vivian Byam Lewes); the residue of her property was left to Charles Lewes, with life annuities to Cara Bray and her house-keeper, Mrs. Dowling.

JOHN Cross moved to Campden Hill in Kensington within a few years and died forty-four years later, on November 3, 1924. He never remarried. Nor did Herbert Spencer ever marry. Until his death at the age of 83 in 1903, he kept a photograph in his bed-room of the woman he had first known as Mary Ann Evans.

In some circles, Cross became a subject of ridicule. Soon after his wife's death he was being called "George Eliot's widow" in London clubs—a veiled reference to what now appears an ambiguous sexual identity. Henry James, who had known Cross before the marriage, visited him at Cheyne Walk and saw him "in his poor wife's empty chair in the beautiful little study they had just made perfect." Cross told Henry James that, as Eliot's husband, he had felt "like a carthorse linked to a racer." The bachelor James's private impression was that "if she had not died, she would have killed him."

Cross showed the depth of his faith in his wife's greatness by completing *George Eliot's Life as Related in Her Letters and*

*Journals* in the four years immediately following her death. Its preface is dated Campden Hill, December 1884, though Cross later noted that in fact he had passed the winter in Cannes, where his old friend Lord Acton, the first reader of the manuscript, had given him "valuable counsel and generous sympathy." It was published in Edinburgh and London in three volumes in 1885, revised and expanded in 1886.

In the twentieth century, Cross's biography was much derided for its censorship of George Eliot's letters and journals. Yet knowing Marian's aversion to biography, how could he have done otherwise? Following her wishes, he destroyed (after combing them for his *Life*) the first forty-six pages of the two-hundred-page journal begun when Marian was in Geneva in 1849. He also obeyed Spencer's direction to make clear that Spencer had not been in love with her and was certainly never informally engaged to her.

But he still had voluminous material to work with, notably Marian's vast correspondence and detailed personal journals. It was a sincere act of respect for the dead to cut out explicit sexual references. He virtually eliminated John Chapman from the story—a strong indication that he had, indeed, been Marian's lover during the two years she lived under his roof at 142 Strand. He also cut out the salutation "Nephew" in all her letters to him.

From her journals, he extracted and included in his *Life* the names of the many books Marian and Lewes had read together in the long evenings in Weimar and Berlin in 1854 and 1855. He extracted, too, some good anecdotes, such as her description of early domestic bliss in Berlin: "How we used to rejoice in the idea of our warm room and coffee as we battled our way from dinner against the wind and snow!" Cross also recorded her account of the 1855 episode when Lewes told her in Richmond Park that her article on Dr. John Cumming had convinced him of true genius in her writing. He drew on his own memories of her explaining her reasons for choosing George Eliot as a pseudonym.

Cross's introductory sketch of Marian's childhood provides most of what is known about her early years, from 1819 to 1838. He was swift to interview people before they disappeared. Chief among these was Isaac Evans, who gave him a clear picture of his sister's childhood life in Nuneaton. From their conversations, Cross learned of the siblings' childhood fishing expeditions, of how the coach passed the gates of Griff House twice a day, and of their father's great physical strength. From Marian's half-sister, Fanny, and her old teacher Maria Lewis, he retrieved information about her early feeling and school experiences that no one else could have supplied.

As widower, Cross had his own store of memories from what Marian had told him, such as her happiness as a child with the book *The Linnet's Life*, which her father had given her, and her misery at Miss Lathom's school when the older girls prevented her getting near the fire. He collected the revealing letters she had written to friends such as Sara Hennell about her personal relations and religious beliefs.

In the second volume of his biography, Cross was open and honest about his wife's connection to Lewes and made clear that not only was Mr. Lewes's previous family life "irretrievably spoiled, but his home had been wholly broken up for nearly two years." This admission shocked many readers, to the dismay of Henry James, who, in February 1885, complained to a friend that although the biography was "full of high decency, earnestness," reviewers were more interested in "the scandalous Bohemian fact that she lived 25 years conjugally with G. H. Lewes without marrying him."

From his conversations with Isaac Evans, Cross also drew the pronouncement, on which subsequent biographers have seized, that "the trait that was the most marked in her all through life [was] the absolute need of some one person who should be all in all to her, and to whom she should be all in all." Without naming himself, Cross clearly felt that of all Marian's loves, he had best met that need.

His biography ends gracefully. Describing her last letter, the unfinished letter of condolence to Mrs. Richard Strachey on the loss of her sister, which Marian had begun on her deathbed, Cross wrote, "The pen which had carried delight and comfort to so many minds and hearts, here made its last mark."

This is hagiography done with love and eloquence. All subsequent biographers owe a debt to this devoted, diligent keeper of the flame. With intelligence and respect, Cross shaped and blended material from vast correspondence and many personal interviews. He left an invaluable portrait of his late wife, the brilliant, depressive autodidact transformed by George Henry Lewes's love into one of the greatest novelists of English literature.

# BIBLIOGRAPHICAL NOTE

As a novelist, George Eliot felt that "Biography is generally a disease of English literature." One of the many ironies of the complicated life of Mary Anne Evans Lewes is that she never imagined it would be offered to posterity by the most meticulous and respectful of scholars. All who have written about her since the mid-1950s have owed a debt to Gordon S. Haight (1901–1985), professor at Yale University, who wrote the revealing *George Eliot and John Chapman* in 1940 and went on to produce, first, an accurate and beautifully annotated nine-volume collection of her letters, and then *George Eliot: A Biography*, published by Oxford University Press in 1968. Today, there is no Eliot without Haight.

In writing this short life of the great Victorian author, I have also been greatly assisted by a book I believe is unfairly criticized: the biography written just after her death by her widower, J. W. Cross, *George Eliot's Life as Related in Her Letters and Journals*. I have been helped also by the perceptive, scholarly, and readable biographies by Kathryn Hughes (*George Eliot: The Last Victorian*, 1998) and Rosemary Ashton (*George Eliot: A Life*, 1993, and *G. H. Lewes: A Life*, 1991) and by Ashton's *142 Strand: A Radical Address in Victorian London* (2006). Both authors have also been a great help in answering questions about the subject of our shared interest.

Retrieving the relevant books has been made possible by the fine services of the London Library and by the incomparable biography store held by the Central Library of the Royal Borough of Kensington and Chelsea. I am grateful also to others: the George Eliot Fellowship, my literary agent Ellen Levine, my editor Annabel Wright, and my friend Bernard McGinley, who read the manuscript in rough draft. Above all, I am indebted to my late husband John, my children Bronwen and Bruno, and my granddaughter Laura—all of whom, in their individual ways, have the gift that was George Eliot's: of delivering a story well told.

# NOTES

## CHAPTER ONE

1. A transparently autobiographical description of the sisters' hair appears in *The Mill on the Floss.*

## CHAPTER TWO

1. The essay, found in a bookshop in Wiltshire in 1943, is reprinted in full in Gordon Haight's *George Eliot: A Biography*, Oxford, 1968, pp. 552–554.

## CHAPTER THREE

1. Charles Darwin had ten children by his wife, Emma, whom he married in 1839. He considered birth control immoral. Janet Browne, *Charles Darwin: The Power of Place*, Princeton University Press, 2003, p. 444.

## CHAPTER FOUR

1. Because she lacked religious belief, she could not get work as a schoolteacher.
2. Eliot biographer Kathryn Hughes has speculated that the letters, which have not been found, warned Marian against getting too close to Chapman.
3. Chapman's diary was found in the 1930s in a shop in Nottingham market and reached Yale University not long after.

4. He did not throw them in the fire. His letters survived along with his diaries, and reached various archives, including those of Yale and the University of Birmingham.

## CHAPTER FIVE

1. Bessie Parkes was the daughter of the Radical Member of Parliament Joseph Parkes, who had subsidized Marian's *Das Leben Jesu* translation, and later the mother of Hilaire Belloc.

## CHAPTER SIX

1. Born in London, Lewes had gone to school in Jersey and Brittany, returned to England to complete his education at a seminary in Greenwich, then taught English in Germany in 1838–1839.
2. These quotes come from Bessie's daughter's recollection of the letter as given to Eliot biographer Gordon Haight in 1942. It is the only account we have of the couple's sex life.

## CHAPTER SEVEN

1. "Sooty skinned" was a reference to Hunt's dark complexion and reputed descent from the oldest settlers in Barbados.
2. As an inducement, Chapman, who was about to resume his abandoned medical training, even suggested that sexual relations might cure Barbara's menstrual problems.

## CHAPTER NINE

1. Opium was fully available over the counter and used as a sedative and pain reliever.
2. *Romola*, chapter 24.

## CHAPTER TEN

1. The inhabitants of the little town of Oberammergau had presented the Passion play every ten years since 1632, when a plague stopped just short of the village.

## CHAPTER ELEVEN

1. Tennyson recorded this description in *A Memoir*.

## CHAPTER TWELVE

1. Had Deronda been identified earlier in the novel as a Jew, Marian could not have had him study at Cambridge, for Jews were not then admitted to Oxford or Cambridge.

## CHAPTER THIRTEEN

1. Rich as she was, she was not in a class with Dickens, who left a total of £93,000 (about $9,700,000 in today's money) when he died, in 1870.

2. Rosemary Ashton, an Eliot biographer, cites a letter from Edward Beesly to Herbert Spencer (Beesly Papers, University College London).

3. Another hint that Marian had been preparing herself for marriage may be found in her letter to Elma Stuart the previous year, which commented favorably on "the fine old houses" on the Chelsea Embankment.

4. This four-story building remains in Venice. Now renovated and renamed the Ca' Giustinian, it is the headquarters of the Venice Biennale and stands at the entrance to the Grand Canal, around the corner from St. Mark's Square. Apart from the addition of new docks and bus stops, it is unchanged in size and shape since Marian and John Cross stayed there.

## CHAPTER FOURTEEN

1. This injustice was remedied a century later when a plaque was placed in the Abbey, on June 21, 1980. Unveiled by Eliot biographer Gordon Haight before seven hundred guests, it was inscribed with a quotation from "Janet's Repentance": "The first condition of human goodness is something to love; the second, something to reverence."

# INDEX